Liberating Minds

Also by Ellen Condliffe Lagemann

A Generation of Women:
Education in the Lives of Progressive Reformers

Nursing History: New Perspectives, New Possibilities

Private Power for the Public Good: A History of the Carnegie
Foundation for the Advancement of Teaching

Jane Addams on Education

The Politics of Knowledge: The Carnegie Corporation,
Philanthropy, and Public Policy

Brown v. Board of Education:
The Challenge for Today's Schools (with LaMar Miller)

Philanthropic Foundations: New Scholarship, New Possibilities

Issues in Education Research:
Problems and Possibilities (with Lee S. Shulman)

An Elusive Science: The Troubling History of Education Research

What Is College For? The Public Purpose of Higher Education
(with Harry Lewis)

Liberating Minds

THE CASE FOR COLLEGE IN PRISON

Ellen Condliffe Lagemann

THE NEW PRESS

25 YEARS

NEW YORK
LONDON

Requests for permission to reproduce selections from this book
should be mailed to: Permissions Department, The New Press,
120 Wall Street, 31st floor, New York, NY 10005.

Published in the United States by The New Press, New York, 2016
Distributed by Perseus Distribution

ISBN 978-1-62097-059-1 (hc)
ISBN 978-1-62097-123-9 (e-book)
CIP data is available

The New Press publishes books that promote and enrich public discussion and
understanding of the issues vital to our democracy and to a more equitable world.
These books are made possible by the enthusiasm of our readers; the support
of a committed group of donors, large and small; the collaboration of our many
partners in the independent media and the not-for-profit sector; booksellers, who
often hand-sell New Press books; librarians; and above all by our authors.

www.thenewpress.com

Composition by dix!
This book was set in Fairfield LH Light

Printed in the United States of America

2   4   6   8   10   9   7   5   3   1

For
the students
of
the Bard Prison Initiative

Of all the civil rights for which the world has struggled and fought for five thousand year, the right to learn is undoubtedly the most fundamental.

—W.E.B. Du Bois, "The Freedom to Learn" (1949)

Contents

Liberating Minds

Introduction

On a hot June day in 2008, I sat with about one hundred other visitors in the yard of the Woodbourne Correctional Facility in upstate New York. We had come for the graduation of the first cohort of students from the Bard Prison Initiative to receive bachelor's degrees. It was an exciting moment because up to this point students in Bard's prison program had earned only associate's degrees. As several student speakers walked to the podium, their classmates cheered, clapped, and yelled encouragement. Each spoke powerfully about the sense of personal efficacy and the intellectual confidence his Bard education had given him. "All I knew before was the street," the first speaker remarked. "I was tied to its rules and expectations. Now I have read Plato and Shakespeare, studied history and anthropology, passed calculus, and learned to speak Chinese. I know the world will be what I make of it. I can make my family proud." They all spoke of their determination to contribute to society. "With this education," another speaker announced, "I not only understand my debt to society, but I am also now in a position to repay it."[1]

While I listened to these well-spoken men and watched them walk up to the president to shake his hand and receive their diplomas, I thought back to the last commencement ceremony I had attended, some years earlier. I was dean of the Harvard Graduate School of Education then, and the ceremony took place in Harvard Yard. As the name of each graduate or professional school was called, its dean would stand up and tip his or her hat to the president and then extol the superb leadership qualifications of his or her students. The students roared their approval and waved something symbolic of their particular school. The ed school students waved children's books; the business school students waved dollar bills.

The two ceremonies were much alike, even though one took place within the wire-topped walls of a prison yard and the other in the shade of Harvard Yard's stately elm trees. The academics in robes, the pomp and circumstance, and the smiling faces of family members were all just the same. But the routes the students had taken to graduation were worlds apart.

The graduates of the Bard Prison Initiative had all been convicted of felonies and were nearing the ends of relatively long sentences. Few had finished high school before being sent to prison, yet all of them had met the full curricular requirements of a regular Bard College bachelor's degree. In their lack of prior schooling, these men were entirely typical of the prison population. The men and women incarcerated in the United States are among the least educated among us. Most have not gone beyond tenth grade.[2] But the Bard graduates are not typical in their post-prison lives. While the national rate of return to prison is over 50 percent, the recidivism rate for graduates of the Bard Prison Initiative is 2 percent, and for those who have taken some classes but did not complete a degree the rate is 5 percent. Most alums of the program move on to good jobs, many in social service agencies and in public health organizations, although graduates have also found jobs in publishing, real estate, and legal services. Many have pursued graduate degrees, including in New York University's master's program in urban planning, Columbia University's master's programs in public health and social work, and Yale University's master's program in divinity.

Recidivism rates for prisoners who have graduated from other college-in-prison programs are comparably impressive. Hudson Link, which offers associate's and bachelor's degrees through several different colleges at five correctional facilities in New York State, reports a return rate of 2 percent.[3] The Cornell University Prison Education Program reports a 7 percent recidivism rate for students who have completed fewer than three courses upon release, and zero percent recidivism for those who have gone on from Cornell to complete an associate's degree.[4] The Prison University Project at San Quentin State Prison, north of San Francisco, reports recidivism rates for its students of 17 percent after three years as opposed to a state rate of 65 percent.[5]

Moving from Harvard to Bard, where I have been deeply involved in the prison program, has demonstrated to me how vitally important it is to offer opportunities to go to college to those who are incarcerated. Today, prisons are schools for crime. They must become schools for citizenship. The Bard program and others around the country offer powerful evidence that most people in prison who earn college degrees are both prepared and highly motivated to return to society and use their talents in positive ways.

Today more and more people are working to make "college for all" a reality in the United States. Doing so is important in helping individuals realize their full potential, which advances not only their personal well-being, but also the greater good of society.

As President Obama has argued on several occasions, ensuring that all men and women complete at least two years of college is critical for the economy. Once the leader of the world in rates of college completion, the United States has slipped markedly in comparison to other countries. Because good jobs today require

high levels of knowledge and skill, the decline in college graduation rates in recent years threatens our economic competitiveness.
So does the fact that there are not enough college graduates to
meet the demands of the labor market. On the positive side of the
ledger, the Commission on Inclusive Prosperity of the Center for
American Progress noted in a 2015 report that even a 1 percent
increase in a state's college graduation rates raises wages for *all*
workers, even high school dropouts, more than 1 percent.[6] In light
of the indisputable role college-going plays in the nation's economic
well-being, Congress is considering legislation that would help fi-
nance at least two years of college, which makes good sense. Other
hopeful signs are financial aid programs in place in a number of
states, including Tennessee and Oregon, as well as in cities such as
Chicago, designed to make college affordable for all students. The
movement to ensure both college access and completion gains adherents every day. It is in the best interests of all of us that people
in prison be included in such plans.

In addition to providing direct economic benefits, college in
prison is cost-effective. The expense of incarceration is stagger-
ing, and by significantly lowering recidivism, thereby reducing the
number of men and women imprisoned, college programs promise to lower the costs substantially. On average, between 2009
and 2015, American taxpayers spent nearly $70 billion a year on
prisons, and due to a dramatic increase in the size of the prison
population and consequent boom in the building of prisons, the
costs have been escalating. According to the National Association
of State Budget Officers, between 1986 and 2012, overall state
spending for corrections increased by 427 percent, from $9.9 bil-
lion to $52.4 billion.[7] The rising cost of prisons is siphoning vital
funding away from more productive uses, including investments
in public education, health care, and infrastructure. Spending on
prisons has come to rank second after health care in its rate of
growth, and that increase has necessitated spending cuts in other

areas. Higher education and K–12 education are among the biggest losers.[8] Reversing the tide, so that less is spent on prisons and more on education, is critical for the nation's economic future. Research indicates that cutting the recidivism rate in state prisons by even 10 percent could save all fifty states combined $635 million from their expenses on corrections—and that does not include the potential savings from reducing recidivism in the extensive federally run prison system.[9]

In addition, college in prison can reduce crime. Estimates suggest that spending $1 million on correctional education, which includes basic adult education, GED instruction, and vocational education as well as more traditional college programs, would prevent 600 crimes from being committed, while spending the same amount on incarceration alone would prevent only 350 crimes.[10] The benefits of reducing crime are manyfold, from alleviating the harm done to victims, to lowering the costs of lost property and bringing down the expense associated with policing and prosecution.

College-in-prison programs have a powerful positive effect on the quality of life inside prisons, both for people in custody and for officers. A large national study by the nonpartisan Commission on Safety and Abuse in America's Prisons confirmed widespread claims that violence is a serious problem in both jails and prisons, perpetrated not only by those who are incarcerated, but also by corrections officers. While officers live in fear of being attacked, men and women in custody, in turn, fear abuse at the hands of officers as well as attacks by those imprisoned with them.[11]

Overcrowding contributes to violence. In 2014, the prison systems of seventeen states imprisoned many more people than they were designed to hold. According to a 2012 report about federal prisons, they, too, are over capacity, by 39 percent. Overcrowding results in double or even triple bunking, waiting lists for education and drug treatment programs, limited work opportunities, and higher inmate to staff ratios, all of which intensifies tensions and leads to flare-ups.[12] By reducing recidivism so dramatically, college programs are a reliable means of alleviating this problem.

Higher education is a powerful antidote to the sense of purposelessness and the intense boredom many of the incarcerated describe in prison memoirs. The poet Dwayne Betts, a recent graduate of Yale Law School, explains that during his eight years in a Maryland prison his "occupation was time."[13] There were apparently no opportunities for education available, although, on his own initiative, Betts found considerable pleasure in reading. The dearth of advanced education is unfortunate for many reasons, not least the fact that college programs are said to give students focus and goals to reach for, which has a positive impact on the atmosphere of a prison.

Many wardens and officers remark upon the improvements in behavior college-in-prison programs can promote. Some participants have confirmed that going to college had a positive effect on their behavior. For example, one woman explained in an interview that when she first arrived at Bedford Hills, where she was being held, she was "a chronic discipline problem." She was often rude and broke many rules. Then, when she enrolled in college, her behavior changed. Because she had something to care about, she became less angry and aggressive and managed to avoid getting in trouble.[14] A study conducted by the Urban Institute to evaluate the effects of college-in-prison programs found that participants had formed supportive associations with other students and were now motivated to avoid conflicts.[15]

The Commission on Safety and Abuse in America's Prisons argues in its report that it is important to create safe and productive environments in correctional facilities not only because it is the just thing to do, but also because "what happens inside jails and prisons does not stay inside jails and prisons. It comes home with prisoners after they are released and with corrections officers at the end of each day's shift."[16] In this way, conditions in prisons affect us all. With more college offerings in prisons, more people would be sent home empowered to become skilled employees, responsible family members, and productive citizens. This would help mitigate the untold "collateral damage" done to families and communities by the incarceration of so many people.

The most direct advantage for families and communities that results from college-in-prison programs is financial. Men and women who go to college in prison are more successful in finding well-paid jobs after they are released. As a result, they are able to provide considerably more financial support for their families. In addition, when men and women leave prison with a college credential, or even just a few college credits, they are more likely to help improve life in their neighborhoods than to contribute again to its dysfunction. Many among those who have been to college in prison are active in community renewal work or activities with young people.[17]

Beyond the direct financial benefit to a family, having a father, mother, or sibling go to college in prison can become a source of pride and inspiration for others in their family. Some family members of people in prison report a keen sense of shame about having a close relative behind bars, and the pride of a son or mother or spouse going to college can help counteract that pain. Imprisoned college students are often the first in their families to seek postsecondary education. Many boast that as a result of their pursuit of advanced education, a relative, maybe a sister or a nephew, is now also enrolled in college. Many also proudly announce that they are asked to help with homework assignments. Students in the Bard Prison Initiative talk constantly of their determination to ensure that their children graduate from high school and move directly to college.

Helping members of the next generation avoid prison is a goal for many incarcerated college students. Such commitments show that, while incarceration is designed to remove prisoners from participation in society, college-in-prison programs can help to kindle a wish to reengage with society in positive ways as well as enhance a student's capacity to do so. If asked about how going to college has empowered them, many respond that the experience has helped them develop the capacity to give back and make restitution for the pain and harm they caused. Researchers who have studied the outcomes of college-in-prison programs have documented these sentiments in interviews. One participant in a college program at the Bedford Hills Correctional Facility for Women told a team of researchers, "After having time to reevaluate how many people were hurt and the ridiculous choices I made . . . the process of going to college [turned] my remorse into wanting to make amends. Wanting to make things better. Helping others not make the same mistakes." [18]

Students also frequently talk about the importance of college classes in teaching them about the way society operates and in helping them understand the complexities of the social conditions in which they grew up. A large number come from impoverished, dangerous neighborhoods, and many come from homes where there has been domestic violence. The new skills and perspectives they gain lead some to pursue work in social services, community development, and criminal justice, often advocating for reform. Their civic engagement can help to heal deep wounds in our society and strengthen our democracy. The Reverend Martin Luther King Jr. once said, "When an individual is no longer a true participant, when he no longer feels a sense of responsibility to his society, the content of democracy is emptied." [19]

At a time of increased attention both to criminal justice reform and to the need for greater access to higher education, this book makes the case for new support for college in prison. College programs were scaled back dramatically in the past few decades. While virtually all state correctional departments offer, or even require, schooling that leads to a general education diploma, and many offer some vocational training and classes designed to prepare people to go home, only a few offer higher education. That is the result of a misguided decision made by Congress, and approved by President Bill Clinton, as part of the 1994 Omnibus Crime Bill, to end Pell Grants for prisoners. The action marked the culmination of several decades of "tough on crime" policies. The Pell Grant program, named after Senator Claiborne Pell, who sponsored the legislation establishing the program, provides need-based grants to low-income students to help them attend college. When prisoners were no longer able to pay for college courses with Pell Grant money, support for college-in-prison programs all but dried up. While in the early 1990s 772 college-in-prison programs operated in 1,287 correctional facilities across the United States, almost all of them were closed down after passage of the 1994 bill.[20]

In recent years, there has been a good deal of critical commentary about the causes and consequences of mass incarceration. The problems with mandatory sentencing have received wide attention, as have the dangers of militarized and discriminatory policing, including "stop and frisk" practices, which have contributed to extremely high rates of incarceration. The appalling conditions that prevail in many prisons are now quite well documented, as is the fact that prisons hold many people with mental illness, which is mostly untreated. But far too little attention has been paid to the great promise of expanding prisoner access to higher education and the many benefits this affords to those who are incarcerated under our current policies, as well as to their families and society at large. That is an egregious oversight that this books aims to correct.

This book draws heavily on research about prison conditions and the effects of incarceration on individuals, families, and communities, as well as the ways college programs can help to combat all of those ills. While not a work of anthropology, the book is grounded in firsthand reports and observations. Since leaving Harvard for Bard, I have spent considerable time teaching and advising in all six of the New York State prisons where Bard operates a college program, and I have gotten to know quite a number of the men and women who are Bard students. I have listened to them talk about their plans for going home. I have also talked with Bard graduates after their release, as they find housing, move into jobs, and continue their education. In addition, I have corresponded or talked with alums and faculty from other college-in-prison programs. But I have included more information gleaned from Bard graduates than from people involved in other college programs. Since most students in the Bard Prison Initiative come from New York City, this gives the book something of both a Bard and a New York orientation, but it has enabled me to write about people and situations I know well. Their stories are told throughout the book in order to ground the discussion in the "real life" experience of individuals who have been to college in prison.

Anthony Cardenales—Tone to his friends—is one of the Bard alumni I write about. He grew up in a poor family in a tough neighborhood in the Bronx, and began stealing food as a child. By the time he was seventeen, he had been convicted of murder. Having earned a bachelor's degree from Bard, in 2009, when he was released, he was able to get a job at a recycling company, where he is still employed and is flourishing. Erica Mateo is another Bard graduate. Her father died less than a year after she was born, and two years later her mother was disabled in a car crash. Though her grandmother stepped in to help raise Erica, she died when Erica was eleven, and Erica was placed in a group home. Soon she was in trouble with the law. In 2002, she was sent to prison for assault. Now she is working for the Center for Court Innovation, developing programs to keep young people in the crime-ridden neighborhood of Brownsville, Brooklyn, from falling into the traps she did.

The stories of Bard graduates like these, and the stories of many other men and women from across the country, are important in communicating the full impact of college in prison. What little writing there is about college programs for people in prison tends to focus on the most easily measured outcomes, primarily rates of return to prison and the employment of students after their release. That is the case, for example, with a widely quoted 2013 RAND Corporation study, *Evaluating the Effectiveness of Correctional Education*, which provides the best available data about the effects of higher education on recidivism.[21] There is no study of which I am aware that addresses such important, if intangible, outcomes as gaining confidence and hope for one's future, feeling excited about making significant contributions to the enrichment of other people's lives, kindling a love of reading or an interest in keeping up with current events, or, most important of all, acquiring the desire and determination to continue learning. The narrow focus of writing about the value of college is true of almost all studies of college-going, including college-going outside of prisons. So much that is important about the college experience, especially in the liberal arts, cannot be captured with the statistical measurement techniques that "hard" science relies upon. Unfortunately, this has helped fuel frequent discounting of the importance of the liberal arts and even of college-going generally. That is why I have relied quite heavily on conversations and firsthand observations, along with memoirs and other written statements by students (sometimes in the form of online journalism).

Controversy over college in prison has been even more heated than the debate about the value of college generally. The tough-on-crime perspective that gained popularity in the United States over the last forty years or so, which led to mandatory long sentences with no chance of parole in addition to the elimination of many work and education programs in prisons, has also fueled criticisms of offering those in prison the chance to attend college. This perspective began to gain standing in the wake of the widespread urban rioting and rise of violence that occurred in the late 1960s and early 1970s. Those promoting tough criminal justice policies stoked public favor in part by arguing that rehabilitation programs

simply did not work, citing research that appeared to support that
view. That research is now recognized as fundamentally flawed,
and today the tide seems to be turning. As I have learned teaching
in the Bard Prison Initiative, our correctional facilities hold many
talented individuals who are eager for more education. New York
governor Andrew Cuomo has recognized this with his plan to expand college programs, as has the Obama administration with its
decision to experiment with reopening Pell eligibility to the incarcerated. More and more people are coming to realize that public
safety is better served by education than by incarceration.

Of course, criticisms concerning the use of taxpayer money
to fund college-in-prison programs continue to draw adherents.
Some people believe that paying for college in prison with tax
funds amounts to favoring the interests of criminals over those
of law-abiding citizens, who are facing onerous financial burdens
due to the rapid escalation of the costs of college. When Governor
Cuomo announced his initiative in 2014 to expand college in prison,
initially proposing that the state legislature help pay for ten college-
in-prison programs, the public backlash was fierce. Cuomo argued
that the programs would likely cut the New York State recidivism
rate by 40 percent, and that with the cost of housing each inmate
running to $60,000 a year in New York the savings would be great.
But a state senator named George D. Maziarz strenuously objected.
"It is simply beyond belief," he said, "to give criminals a competitive edge in the job market over law-abiding New Yorkers who forgo
college because of the high cost." A "Kids Before Cons" online petition appeared on the Internet, featuring a photograph of a group of
white students throwing their caps in the air after graduation, next
to one of convicts in orange prison jumpsuits, who were all people of
color. Under the photo of the white students, a tagline read, "Studied hard. Worked summer jobs. Saved. Took out loans." The tagline
under the photo of the convicts read, "Stole a car. Robbed a bank.
Shot a bystander. Got a free college education paid for by YOU."[22]

The argument was terribly shortsighted. Among other things, it failed to account for the fact that the savings could be directed to grants to assist the many students who have studied hard but cannot afford to attend college. Unfortunately, however, Cuomo had not made that case, and in response to the racially charged campaign, he dropped his original proposal. Remaining convinced of the value of college in prison, however, he announced a new plan early in 2016 that would fund some college-in-prison programs in part from the money brought into state coffers from criminal settlement fines and in part from privately donated funds. Announcing the new plan, he stated, "Prisons were not supposed to be warehouses. It was not supposed to be [that] we're going to take you and put you in a warehouse for ten years and lock you up, and then take you out in ten years and return you to society and think maybe you're going to be better for it."[23] As Cuomo suggested, far too many of those who are sent to prison return home without the knowledge and skills that can lead to gainful employment and rounded, successful lives.

Including college in prison in plans for "college for all" will not only create benefits for the country as a whole, but will also be in keeping with the traditions of expanding education opportunity that have played such an important role in fostering the development of this country. Throughout the nation's history, more and more Americans have had access to education, and this has been especially evident in higher education. In the seventeenth and eighteenth centuries, college was generally restricted to white men preparing to be ministers, lawyers, or doctors. During the Civil War, passage of the Morrill Land Grant Act established agricultural and mechanical colleges throughout the United States, broadening the purpose of higher education as well as enrollment. Colleges for women and for African Americans opened soon thereafter, as did the great research universities, some of which, like Johns Hopkins, were new, and some of which, notably Harvard and Columbia, were colleges transformed through the addition of graduate and professional schools. The great innovation during the twentieth century was the community college, which made access to at least two years of higher education virtually universal. Increasing financial aid was another major step, first with the Servicemen's Readjustment Act (1944), followed by the National Defense Education Act (1958), and finally the Basic Educational Opportunities Act, passed in 1972, which made Pell Grants available to all students who meet the income cutoff.

So many people in prison were locked up at young ages and never received the high-quality schooling we all deserve. Having missed out on so much, many are hungry for ideas, information, and intellectual engagement. They need opportunities to grow and develop their considerable potential. I hope this book will make clear why that is so important—not only for the people being educated, but for all of us—and how that goal can be achieved.

1

Learning to Learn

An Outcome of College in Prison

Joe Williams was born in Brooklyn, New York, on February 16, 1979. His parents were teenagers. After he was born, his mother moved through a series of fairly well-paying jobs. She worked as a receptionist and a corrections officer and then joined the army, obtaining the rank of E-4 Specialist. From there, she moved on to a position as a supervisor for the Metropolitan Transit Authority. According to Joe, his father went in a different direction, becoming "a career criminal and drug abuser." He was in and out of prison, and not around most of the time, and was shot and killed in an ambush intended for Joe. Joe carries his father's picture on his phone to this day.

Although as a youngster he was exposed to crime and neighborhood violence, Joe has many happy memories from his childhood, growing up in a large extended family as the oldest child and grandchild on both sides. On his mother's side, he has one younger sister; on his father's side, he has "too many [siblings] to know how many for certain." He has stayed in touch with the four youngest. His happiest childhood memories involve playing with cousins, especially on Christmas morning, when, he fondly recalls, the kids would spy on the adults as they wrapped the presents.

During summer vacations, the family would pile into someone's car and drive all the way to North Carolina for family reunions; they would stay for a few days and then pile back into the car for the return trip to Brooklyn.

Joe's experience at school produced few good memories. For one thing, he attended several different schools, starting elementary school at Pilgrim Christian Academy in Bushwick and then being transferred to P.S. 298 in Brownsville. Thereafter, he went to two different junior high schools. At William McKinley Junior High School in Bay Ridge, he started getting into fights and stealing from students he had seen acting as bullies to weaker kids. He got kicked out of that school and went to George Gershwin Intermediate School 166 in East New York, where he also got into trouble. Although he was not kicked out, he was not allowed to graduate with his class. He was promoted nonetheless and moved on to Thomas Jefferson High School, also in East New York, which he says was "one of the worst high schools in Brooklyn" at the time. There, he continued to get into trouble and was again kicked out. His grandmother then enrolled him in a GED program, which he completed just before turning sixteen.

As Joe describes his school experience, it was at best a minor interruption in his "real life." He spent most of his time selling drugs, writing rap songs, smoking marijuana, and "just generally scheming about ways to make it out of poverty for my family and me." He was about twelve when he committed his first crime, painting a cap gun black and using it to commit a robbery. He started selling drugs when he was thirteen, and by his fourteenth birthday he "was hustling full time, committing crimes daily." This resulted in a number of arrests and convictions, with time spent locked up for a couple of months at Spofford, a juvenile facility in Hunts Point; then for a month at the Rikers Island jail; and finally, for four years, in a New Jersey state prison on charges of trafficking drugs and guns across state lines. At the age of twenty-four, he began what he describes as his "final stint" in prison, serving a sentence of just under eleven years in New York State, mostly in maximum-security prisons.

Joe says that during the first years of this sentence he did a lot of thinking about who he was and wanted to be and what he needed to do in order to go home ready to establish "a legitimate life for himself and his family." Things started to look up when he landed a job as a peer facilitator for the Transitional Services Center at the Clinton Correctional Facility. That job convinced him that he wanted to work in counseling when he was released. But to be eligible for that kind of work, he knew he would have to get a college degree. In 2007, an opportunity to do that opened up. Having been moved to the Eastern Correctional Facility, one of the places where the Bard Prison Initiative operates, Joe applied and was admitted. By the time he was released from prison in August 2013, he had earned both an associate's and a bachelor's degree. "My decision to pursue a college degree had to do with my strategic planning for my release," he explains.

By being so deliberate in planning his postprison life, after returning home to live with his mother and stepfather, Joe soon landed a job as a checkout clerk at a takeout lunch place in Midtown Manhattan. As a college graduate, he was overqualified for the position, but he stuck with it so he could concentrate on returning to school to earn a master's in social work. He was admitted to the accelerated program in social work policy at the Columbia University School of Social Work and began the program in January 2014, only months after his release from prison. He graduated in May 2015, having accumulated over $100,000 in debt, and moved right into a position as a civil justice social worker at Brooklyn Defender Services. Joe had interned there as a youth advocate while at Columbia and has now helped several of his college classmates also get jobs working with that agency.

Joe is confident he will never go back to prison. But he has not found going straight easy. He once remarked that for someone who has really "lived in high style," a good but relatively modest salary is a serious adjustment. He knows, though, that he is building a solid life and that his work is helping him realize his ambition to take his life in a positive direction. He has married a New York City public school teacher and is actively involved with the one child he had before going to prison, a daughter whom he calls his "butterfly princess," and he and his wife now also have an infant son. He is determined that his children will finish high school, go on to college, and maybe even follow in his footsteps, not to prison, but to graduate school.

Joe's determination comes through emphatically when he speaks about realizing that going to college "was what I knew I needed to succeed" for himself and his family. Once he went to prison, "trouble was *not* an option," he says. It would interfere with his plan to leave prison prepared for a new life. He participated in what he describes as a few "peripheral" activities that would enhance his résumé, including learning American Sign Language, volunteering in the Youth Assistance Program, and earning a certificate in food handling. To stay in shape, he played football and lifted weights, and for his spiritual well-being he became a devout Christian. But once he started college, that became his primary focus, and his commitment to studying hard paid off with a 3.5 grade-point average.

Joe Williams's story demonstrates what can happen when people are given a second chance to obtain a high-quality education. College classes awakened a thirst for knowledge in him and opened his eyes to new ideas. He reports that he was fascinated by the insights he gained from several psychology classes as well as from a new understanding of American history. A social studies major, he especially "loved the classes that expounded on the social construction of race and the development of the systems that strategically were put in place to keep my people ostracized from power." He says that being held to a high academic standard was vital in igniting his passion for learning, and he notes, "People tend to think that incarcerated individuals are not intellectuals. However, the faculty at Bard expected, required, and would not settle for anything less than our best. As incarcerated students, we internalized their belief in us, which we might not have developed on our own, from our own previous accomplishments, especially those relating to academia."[1]

Joe's experience powerfully illustrates the wide range of positive outcomes for students who go to college in prison. In recent years, much of the discussion concerning the purposes of higher education has focused on the economic payoffs not only for the individual, due to improved employment prospects, but for the country as a whole, due to the increasing number of jobs requiring college-level education. The same economic focus has dominated arguments for college for all. Even though economic security is a vitally important outcome of a college education, as longtime Harvard president Derek Bok has argued, a narrow focus on economic payoffs has tended to obscure an important set of additional benefits, which Joe's account underscores. As Bok describes the purposes of college, it should impart "useful knowledge," prepare people for "enlightened" citizenship, and ready them to live a "full and satisfying life."[2] To believe that college is solely about preparing people to get good jobs is to adopt a "shrunken conception of the role of higher learning," Bok maintains, one that "ignores what were long regarded as the most essential aims of education: strengthening students' moral character and preparing them to be active, informed citizens."[3] In a similar vein, former Princeton president Harold T. Shapiro argues that what matters most about the college experience "is not simply what we teach, or even what our students learn, but what kind of persons they become."[4] Expanding on the same theme, moral philosopher Martha C. Nussbaum has observed that college learning can and should promote the capacity to question and reflect on oneself and one's society,

cultivating the ability to see oneself in relation to other human beings around the world and to put oneself in others' shoes, thereby
nurturing a person's full humanity.[5]

While arguments such as these have historically supported the
value of a traditional liberal arts education, today they apply to postsecondary education generally. The National Leadership Council
for Liberal Education, a group convened by the Association of
American Colleges and Universities, emphasized in a report on college learning that there are "recommended learning outcomes" that
"can and should be achieved through many different programs of
study and in all collegiate institutions, including colleges, community colleges and technical institutes, and universities, both public and private." The council, on which both Bok and Nussbaum
served, also offered a clear delineation of the benefits college can
provide: "expanding horizons, building understanding of the wider
world, honing analytical and communication skills, and fostering
responsibilities beyond self."[6]

As college-for-all advocates argue, these benefits are clearly important for everyone. For people in prison, they can be especially
significant because so many of the incarcerated have not had positive prior experiences with education. Many had no expectation of
being able to go to college, and many discover talents they did not
know they had, in the process learning to learn at a high level, and
finding that they enjoy the challenge. Joe's comments about the
importance of being held to high standards express the value he
found in having to push himself to the limit.

The importance of enabling people in prison to discover their
competence as learners is underscored by the glaring gap in educational achievement that exists between those who are incarcerated
and the general population. Forty-one percent of people in custody
in state and federal prisons and in local jails are high school dropouts, compared to 18 percent among the general population. Only
14.4 percent of those serving time in state prisons reported having

some postsecondary education, as opposed to 51 percent of adults in the nonincarcerated U.S. population.[7] There are a variety of reasons for this gap. Many people in prison grew up in neighborhoods with schools so inadequate that they have been labeled "failing," with some having been taken over by the state to be reconstituted. Such schools are known not only for their poor test scores, but often also for their severe suspension policies, commonly known as "zero tolerance" policies. They expel far too many students and this is especially true for African American boys.

Many of those who end up in prison also lacked the close parental supervision and experience of reading at home or listening to stories that have so much to do with developing a joy of learning and achieving school success. Research by sociologist Annette Lareau of the University of Pennsylvania, among others, has provided strong evidence that parenting styles play an important role in school outcomes, and that parenting styles of poor and working-class families tend to differ significantly from those of the middle class. In her book *Unequal Childhoods*, Lareau reports the results of a study of eighty-eight families from different income levels, parental employment, races, and neighborhoods. Her analysis shows that the children of poor and working-class parents generally have more unstructured time, during which parents do not closely supervise them, whereas the children of middle-class parents are scheduled more often to participate in activities. Middle-class parents were also found to engage in more conversation with their children, and impressed upon them the importance of success in school.[8] However indirectly, all this contributes to differences in rates of incarceration.

Significant numbers of men and women in prison have also spent time in foster care or group homes, and many were abused as children. A study of the prior lives of the students who have participated in the Freedom Education Project Puget Sound, which offers college to women incarcerated at the Washington Correction

Center for Women, found that 78 percent of the women had been victims of domestic abuse or childhood sexual or physical abuse.[9] Many became mothers as young teenagers. Another study, published by the U.S. Department of Justice, reported that one-third of all women in state prisons or jails had been abused as children. The percentage is lower for men, but for both men and women, childhood abuse among the incarcerated is roughly twice as high as for the nonincarcerated population.[10] These challenges in the early lives of so many of the incarcerated have much to do with why they either performed poorly in school or had disciplinary problems that undermined their learning. Even students who like going to school and do well are sometimes pulled away by the challenging situations of their lives.

Of course, many of those who are in prison chose to drop out of school, or were forced out, because they had already gotten in trouble with the law. Sometimes a parent, or an uncle, sibling, or cousin, leads a child into selling drugs or some other criminal activity. One college student recollected his mother sending him to work for an uncle who was selling drugs. He was only twelve years old at the time, but his mother needed the money he could earn to support her drug habit. He was eventually arrested and sent to prison. Ironically, after he enrolled in college, when his mother came to visit, she apparently would tell him that he was finally improving, as if she had not played a role in his situation.[11] Friends or older acquaintances from one's neighborhood or fellow gang members are often guides into crime. For some young people, schools, even good ones, are no competition for the street.

The negative school experiences, and negative attitudes about school, that many of the incarcerated developed might be expected to cause a lack of interest in college. But in spite of all the difficulties and choices that impaired school success for so many of them earlier in their lives, men and women in prison are often extremely eager to attend college and want to overcome their prior negative experiences with education. Almost all of the small number of degree-granting prison college programs in existence today are oversubscribed. Even with a selective admission process, requiring candidates to take a challenging written essay exam and submit to an interview, Bard has an applicant-to-admittance ratio of ten to one. Often students must apply several times before gaining entrance, which requires courage as well as persistence, and for those who fail to gain entrance, it is a tough embarrassment since it is widely known throughout the facility who has sat for the exam and who was granted an interview. Other postsecondary programs that have selective admissions also have astounding ratios of applicants to admitted students. Among the seventy men who attended the initial selection meeting for the Prison Entrepreneurship Program in Texas, fifty ultimately sought entrance, though only a handful could be admitted. At programs such as the Prison University Project at San Quentin that are not selective, admitting students on a first-come, first-served basis, the ratios of those who want to participate to those enrolled are also high and there are long waiting lists.

In fact, some college-in-prison programs were launched in response to organizing by incarcerated individuals. That was the case, for example, with the college program at Bedford Hills Correctional Facility for Women in Westchester, New York. There, following the termination of Pell Grant eligibility for prisoners, college programs were discontinued, which apparently resulted in "a feeling of despair . . . as the women experienced a loss of hope about their own futures and the futures of younger women coming into the prison."[12] In response, seven women formed themselves into what they called the "Inmate Committee" to work with the superintendent, who was sympathetic to their wish to reestablish college opportunities. Other administrators, and civilian allies on the outside, helped raise private funds to replace the public monies that were no longer available.

A statement issued by the Inmate Committee captures both the eagerness and the political savvy with which the women pressed their case for reopening the doors to college. "We understand the public's anger about crime and realize that prison is first and foremost a punishment for crime. But we believe that when we are able to work and earn a higher-education degree while in prison, we are empowered to truly pay our debts to society by working toward repairing some of what has been broken. . . . It is for all these reasons, and in the name of hope and redemption, that we ask you to help rebuild a college program here at Bedford Hills Correctional Facility." Winning the support of government officials and community leaders, the Inmate Committee was also able to gain assistance from the president of Marymount Manhattan College, which became the degree-granting institution for a college program that taps faculty from a number of different institutions. Beginning with the reinstatement of a bachelor's degree program in sociology in the spring of 1997, advanced education again found a place in this prison.[13]

The thoughtful insights that students offer about why they have benefited so much from college speak powerfully about the positive attitudes they have developed about learning. When asked in interviews about the value of their classes, former college-in-prison students state again and again that they learned to think more clearly and to see possibilities for themselves they had never known about or believed in before. "I'm a thinker now," a college student at the Bedford Hills Correctional Facility for Women told a team of researchers. "Before I was a reactor. . . . If you're educated and you are well informed about a lot of things, you have a tendency to look at life through a whole different perspective. You have the skills, you have the education. It makes you qualified."[14] Kenny Johnson, who had been a student in the Education Justice Project, a college-in-prison program run by the University of Illinois, stated that "when I first got incarcerated, I had a ninth grade education. I had a limited vision of the world. I had a 'ghetto mentality,' a 'get-them-before-they-get-you' type of attitude." Going to college changed that. It "broadens your horizons," he observed. "Instead of being stuck in tunnel vision, it opens this world up for you."[15] Jorge Heredia, a student in the Prison University Project at San Quentin, described the impact a social psychology class had: "The word 'psychology' used to sound to me as something supernatural. . . . I thought it was useful only for insane people." Now he believes it's for "everyone, because once you take it, you'll be able to save yourself countless conflicts in the environment around you."[16]

The thrill of having learned to learn pervades students' comments. Speaking of his time in college at the program run by Cornell University, a student explained that he loved that "I was being introduced to new concepts that excited my mind. The more I learned, the more I realized just how little I knew."[17] A student in the Bard program remarked at the end of his first semester that he had never imagined that he could master college work. "But apparently I'm smart," he said. "In Bard they see something in me that I didn't see and they want to help us learn."[18] A graduate of the Notre Dame–Holy Cross College program at the Westville Correctional Facility in Indiana spoke in a commencement speech about the value of his studies, noting: "Molding the next generation's thinkers . . . is noble in a traditional college arena, but it is even more crucial here, in prison. We may be here because we have had a lapse, or even a complete lack of using our minds fruitfully to achieve a goal society deems amenable. I know I can continue to use the tenets I have been taught here to better myself and my family. . . . I can spend the last part of my life doing something that benefits society in a new, more important way."[19]

One of the best summations of the energy and commitment incarcerated students bring to their studies can be found in comments made by Rashawn Hughes, a former Bard student, in an interview for National Public Radio. Rashawn took classes while incarcerated at the Eastern Correctional Facility, a maximum-security prison in the Catskills region of New York. He was then transferred to a lower security facility, which would generally be considered a very good thing, but that institution did not offer college classes. When asked if he would go back to Eastern if he could in order to continue his college work, even though he had more freedom at the new facility, he responded, "I would go right after this interview. If they packed me up, tell me, 'Let's go.' I would go right now."[20]

Professors who teach in college-in-prison programs also often speak with great enthusiasm about the eagerness of their students and their willingness to work extremely hard. When Professor Tabetha Ewing, who teaches at Bard, was asked if she had had to make a course easier for the students in the prison, her response was quite to the contrary. "Once I was there three weeks, I . . . made it harder."[21] The students studied even harder than those she had taught before on Bard's main campus. My own experience as a faculty member teaching history classes in the Bard Prison Initiative has been similar. Even though I have not made the courses I have taught more difficult, I have not made them any easier either. I have simply used the syllabi I used previously at Harvard, NYU, and Columbia. What is different is that, in anticipation of class discussions, I think even more intently about the significance of the material, knowing that at least one student will say, "Well, this is all very interesting, but why does it really matter?" Those questions are reflections of serious engagement along with a deep desire to understand fully the insights to be gained from history, which, as a historian, I find not only admirable but also quite gratifying.

Joshua Miller is the executive director of a college program that sends Baltimore-area professors into the Jessup Correctional Institute to teach classes. He reports that students at Jessup "keep on showing up, even though they get nothing for it," since the classes do not carry credit toward degrees. He also remarks, "You're used to teaching classes where the students would rather be sleeping off their hangovers, [but] these guys are desperate to sit in the room and talk with you about big ideas."[22]

Daniel Berthold, one of Bard's most distinguished teachers and a world-class philosopher who has taught in the prison program almost since its inception, has found that his incarcerated students have a "hunger" for understanding and a "passion and sense of need" to know that he has never encountered teaching at Bard's main campus or at any of the other colleges where he has served. He has written that, thanks to his incarcerated students, he has found "wisdom," because he has been able to be a "witness—in the lives of these inmates, who know much better than I ever did that there is indeed a tremendous importance in studying philosophy." They understand, he insists, that engaging with philosophy "can make us free, can redeem us by the way we enact it, practice it, live it."[23] Berthold and others who have taught in college-in-prison programs have found that teaching in the prisons can be transformative—not only for the students, but perhaps even more so for the faculty. It can revivify one's sense of mission and purpose, while also being intellectually challenging, exciting, and fun. Students are ready to turn ideas inside out, to ask difficult questions, to read beyond the pages required, to discuss a class with their friends, and to engage fully and in a rounded fashion with the subjects before them. Most of the students work extremely hard on their papers and other assignments and thoughtfully mull over comments, often asking to rewrite a paper even when doing so will not raise a grade. It is exciting to witness their growth, especially their increasing confidence in their capacity to articulate complicated concepts and points of view.

Of course, it must be noted that not all of those who are sent to prison had poor prior school experiences, or particularly tough home lives. Sometimes people who were quite good in school and really enjoyed it, and who grew up in comfortable, stable homes, also become involved in activities that take them off the path to college. For them, the role of college in prison is to reignite their commitment to learning and inspire them to get back to a productive life. Such is the case for Wesley Caines, who, after his release from a twenty-five-year sentence, got a job with the Brooklyn Defender Services.

Wes was born in St. Thomas, in the U.S. Virgin Islands, in 1966. His parents were both from the Caribbean, his father from St. Kitts and his mother from Antigua; they emigrated to New York City when he was in elementary school. He grew up in the northeast Bronx, where he lived with his mother, who worked as a domestic and nursing assistant, after his parents divorced. Then, when he was twelve or thirteen, she remarried and moved to Florida and he moved in with his father, who worked for a wholesale textile distribution company. Wes says that he "loved school!" and that his family expected him to do well. They made him spend time reading every day before he could go out to play sports with his friends. He earned high grades, and when he was in high school, in addition to playing several sports, he also helped his father with his business. He was a hardworking, successful, and happy young man.

But despite this solid start in life, Wes became involved in criminal activity before he had finished high school. Then, while enrolled as a student at SUNY Farmingdale, he was arrested on a felony murder charge and began his long sentence. When Bard arrived in the prison where he was in custody, he says he jumped at the chance "to reengage in my academic pursuits." After completing an associate's degree, he moved on to a bachelor's, which he completed in 2009. He maintained an A average throughout and distinguished himself with his professors as a leader among his peers. They admired his quiet, clear way of participating in class discussions and his willingness to help others who were less advanced or less academically savvy. They also were impressed by his independence of mind and especially his willingness to defend conservative ideas in a college culture that was distinctly liberal.

Wes was a member of the first class I taught in the Bard Prison Initiative. From the first session of that class to the last, he was my tutor in what to expect—bells sounding at odd times and students being pulled out of classes by officers for unexplained reasons. He seemed to understand intuitively that a "civilian volunteer" like me needed help figuring out the norms of prison teaching. It was thanks to Wes's tutelage that within a week of beginning to teach I felt entirely comfortable in this new setting and was able to enjoy the lively curiosity students brought to our discussions.

Soon after I met Wes, who had earned his bachelor's degree just before I arrived, he applied for entrance to the New York Theological Seminary's master's program in professional studies. When he was accepted, he was transferred to Sing Sing for a year, since that was the only facility where the program was offered. As a result, I only heard through the grapevine that he was doing exceptionally well. That was not surprising to me, since Wes is a talented writer and thinks and argues very clearly. Months after earning his master's, Wes was paroled and allowed to return home to his family in the Bronx. His college degrees assured his employers that he was up to the job they offered, in which he is now excelling. He has been asked to plan and implement a reentry program for other formerly incarcerated people returning home. Wes is giving back to his community in other ways as well, notably through his work on the board of the Brooklyn Community Bail Fund, which loans bail money (up to $2,000) to people who cannot come up with the funds they need to avoid time in jail.[24]

Going to college in prison has been instrumental to the success of many other formerly incarcerated men and women. The strong reasoning and communication skills individuals such as Joe Williams and Wes Caines have developed have impressed employers and helped them to overcome the stigma of having been incarcerated. Their broadened perspectives and richer understanding of society and of how they can make significant contributions are helping them succeed not only in their work but also in other aspects of their lives as family members and community leaders. Because they have learned to learn at high levels, they are likely to continue learning, which can offer many advantages and much happiness for years to come.

2

Of Value to All

The Economics of College in Prison

Anthony Cardenales, who is usually just called Tone, was convicted of murder at the age of seventeen and sentenced to seventeen years in prison. During that time, he earned both an associate's and a bachelor's degree from Bard, which enabled him to land a job immediately after his release at the WeRecycle firm in Mount Vernon, New York, now known as Hugo Neu Recycling. His college experience also helped him learn all he needed to know to take on increasing responsibility, and today he is vice president for administration at the company. Going to college changed his views about learning, which had not excited him growing up.

Tone's life story was featured in the book *Random Family: Love, Drugs, Trouble, and Coming of Age in the Bronx,* by Adrian Nicole LeBlanc, in which he is referred to by the pseudonym César. The book vividly depicts the challenges of coming of age in a poor, troubled neighborhood, where the likelihood of being drawn into crime is high. When Tone was growing up in the South Bronx around Tremont Avenue, the neighborhood's poverty and physical devastation were notorious. During an electrical blackout in the borough in the summer of 1977, when he was two, people looted the shops along Tremont and set fires that tore through the community.

When yet another fire raged out of control that fall during the second game of the World Series, being played at nearby Yankee Stadium, sportscaster Howard Cosell is said to have announced: "Ladies and gentlemen, the Bronx is burning." The series of fires left the neighborhood looking as though it had been bombed. In the ensuing years, gang violence and drugs, mostly heroin and crack cocaine, plagued the community. In the words of *New York Times* photojournalist David Gonzales, who also grew up there, the South Bronx became a "brand name for urban decay and despair."[1]

Tone's father was addicted to drugs and did not see much of his son. His mother did not have a regular paying job. She had been taking care of children for most of her life, starting as a child who was responsible for her siblings and then raising her own four children. The family relied on welfare and handouts from her boyfriends to pay the rent and buy food and to supply her with cocaine when she was using. By the end of each month, Tone and his siblings had little to eat, and early on he started snitching fruit from the nearby Korean grocery to ease his hunger.

As he grew up, Tone spent much of his time with three close friends, roaming the streets, jumping across rooftops, and spraying buildings and subway cars with graffiti. Before long they shifted to selling drugs, carrying guns, and assaulting and robbing people along Fordham Avenue, a major Bronx thoroughfare, as well as in the subway. Though his mother tried to discipline him, sometimes even beating him, he persisted. Uninterested in school, he dropped out in seventh grade. He was sent to a juvenile detention facility twice, but that did not deter him from getting into trouble. After being convicted of attempted murder, he was sentenced to two to six years in the Harlem Valley Secure Center for juvenile offenders in Wingdale, New York, fifty miles from New York City. As a condition of his release, the court ordered that he attend classes at Bronx Community College, but he quickly lost interest and dropped out, again selling drugs.[2] He started on a new course only years later, while he was serving his seventeen-year murder sentence. His then eight-year-old daughter came to visit him in prison one day, during a time when he was being held in solitary confinement for getting into fights. He had been told that his daughter was also getting into trouble for fighting, and when he admonished her to try to control herself and not fight, she responded, "But that's what you do, you get into fights, Daddy."[3] That helped him see what a negative impact his behavior was having on his daughter, which inspired him to embark on a decade-long journey toward his bachelor's degree. He first took college courses offered by the New York Theological Seminary at the Shawangunk Correctional Facility in Ulster County, New York. Then, in 2003, he was moved to the Woodbourne Correctional Facility in bordering Sullivan County, which is one of the prisons where the Bard Prison Initiative operates. He applied, was admitted, and did very well, graduating in 2008, thereby fulfilling his wish to show his daughter that he could accomplish important, difficult things.

Upon his release, his first job at WeRecycle was as a project coordinator, which required him to master the complexities involved in taking apart computers and televisions. He knew nothing about electronics recycling when he started, but due to his success in college, he was confident that he could learn. He performed well and was soon promoted and given responsibility for organizing the work of all the men employed on the plant floor. In less than six years, he was promoted five times, moving up through various departments; now he is one of the company's most senior managers. Today, he is earning enough to help support his five children as well as other members of his family. He has also been able to assist other people coming home from prison, even finding some of them jobs working with him at the recycling firm.

Almost all people in prison are released at some point, and reentering society after time away is extremely challenging. The obstacles those released from prison face are daunting. In some states, for example, formerly incarcerated men and women are not eligible for food stamps and cannot reside in public housing. In addition, the vast majority of people released from prison must meet with a parole officer regularly for at least several years to report on their activities and in some cases be tested for drugs. Finding work is the highest hurdle, and is often a long, arduous, and dispiriting experience.

One reason work is so hard to find is that so many people coming home from prison are returning to poor, struggling urban communities where there are few jobs. In addition, they almost always face negative attitudes on the part of employers. One 2003 study found that only 12.5 percent of the employers surveyed were even willing to entertain job applications from people who had been to prison.[4] Glenn E. Martin, who served a six-year prison term and is now president of JustLeadershipUSA, an advocacy group working on issues related to incarceration, has written thoughtfully about this problem. When men and women leave prison, he says, they enter a new prison, a "prison of stigma."[5] Devah Pager, a Harvard sociologist who studies racial discrimination in employment, echoes this point, noting that ex-offenders looking for work are "marked."[6]

Due to intense lobbying by advocates of criminal justice reform, over one hundred cities and counties and twenty-four states have recently passed so-called ban the box laws (and more are doing so all the time), which prohibit employers from asking job seekers on applications whether they have been convicted of a crime.[7] However, in this day of ready access to personal information, employers can easily find out whether an applicant has a criminal record.

Of course, another reason that men and women returning home from prison have great difficulty finding jobs is that they lack the knowledge, skill, confidence, and positive outlook, in addition to the credentials, needed to secure them. As Dora B. Schriro, a former corrections commissioner in Arizona, Missouri, and New York

City, commented to a reporter, people in prison are generally "released no better than when they went in—and as likely to return."[8]

The result is that many of those coming home remain unemployed for long periods or are only able to find part-time or un-
skilled, low-wage work. A study conducted by the Ella Baker
Center for Human Rights in 2014 found that almost two-thirds
of those released from prison were unemployed or underemployed
after five years.[9] What is more, the economic impact of incarceration is not limited to the period of imprisonment and the prolonged
time it may take to find work; it often persists over the course of
a formerly incarcerated person's entire working life. The earning
capacity of people who have been to prison is significantly diminished. Potential income is lost during incarceration and the average
total income earned by men who have been to prison by the time
they are forty-eight years old is 41 to 50 percent lower than for men
who have never been to prison.[10]

Men and women who have been to college while in prison face all
the same obstacles upon release, but they are much better prepared
to cope with them than their noncollege peers. Not only do their
college credentials help them find work, but the self-assurance and
hopefulness they often gain can bolster their resilience in the face
of sometimes daunting challenges. Going to college also instills
discipline, which helps graduates meet parole obligations, show up
on time reliably once jobs are found, work vigorously, and pay bills
on time and meet the general requirements of life on the outside.

For the college-in-prison programs that are tracking outcomes,
the employment results are impressive. Jed Tucker, director of
reentry for the Bard Prison Initiative, cautions that it is difficult
to generate solid employment statistics at any given point in time
because recently released graduates often move from job to job
for a period of months or even years before settling into suitable
long-term placements. That said, the tracking he has done shows

that approximately 75 percent of Bard's alums find work within a month of arriving home. The alumni coordinator for Hudson Link for Higher Education in Prison, which operates a college program at Sing Sing and a number of other New York State prisons, reports an astonishing 95 percent employment rate among the almost 400 former students who have been released.[11]

It is also noteworthy that those who secure good jobs are likely to hold on to them because they perform exceptionally well. Lisa Schreibersdorf, the executive director of Brooklyn Defender Services, who has hired a number of former college-in-prison students, is so happy with their performance that she says she would hire twenty more if she could. She believes they work harder than other people because they want to overcome their histories.[12] The director of human resources for an engineering firm outside of New York City agrees. He reports that in his firm the employees with the lowest turnover and highest rates of promotion are those with "criminal backgrounds who've completed college degrees." They have, he says, "the highest potential, demonstrated commitment, adaptability and what we call 'hunger'—a consciousness of having the highest risk of being overlooked or underestimated, and therefore the highest stake in their success."[13]

Good jobs yield direct economic benefits to the employees involved as well as to their families, and providing access to college to many more of the incarcerated would be likely to yield significant public payoffs. One enormous public cost that could be significantly alleviated is the burden of the high unemployment among the formerly incarcerated. With more than 650,000 men and women released from U.S. prisons every year, the economic impact nationwide of having so many men and women unable to find work is considerable. One study seeking to quantify the impact estimated that the national unemployment rate among working-age males in 2008 was increased—by 1.5 to 1.7 percent—due to the number of formerly incarcerated men who were unemployed, and that the cost to the U.S. economy of that lowered employment was between $57 and $65 billion in lost output.[14] Rather than acting as a drain on the economy, those who find work when they return home from prison become contributors of tax revenue to federal, state, and local treasuries.

Another substantial economic benefit would come from the reduction in recidivism. The low rates of return to prison among people who have been to college in prison are striking in comparison to the high overall rate of recidivism. A widely cited study conducted by the U.S. Bureau of Justice Statistics found that among more than 400,000 people released from state correctional facilities in thirty states in 2005, 30 percent were arrested again within six months of release, 67.8 percent were rearrested within three years of release, and the number rose to 76.6 percent five years after release.[15] Recall that for both Bard and Hudson Link, by comparison, the recidivism rate for people who have earned associate's or bachelor's degrees is just 2 percent as of this writing; and for those who earn an associate's degree from Cayuga Community College after Cornell classes in prison, the rate is zero.

Several other programs also report impressive reductions in recidivism. The Prison Entrepreneurship Program in Texas is one that has seen good results. It sends selected inmates to the Cleveland Correctional Center in Cleveland, Texas, for a mixture of classes in business administration and entrepreneurship along with hands-on counseling and training by entrepreneurs and business leaders. The aim is to assist graduates in starting their own businesses after release. A study conducted by the Baylor Institute for Studies of Religion showed that the program reduces recidivism from 24 percent to 6 percent.[16] For classes that have been taught for several decades by Boston University professors at prisons in Massachusetts, Professor James F. Gilligan reports that not one of the students has returned to prison over a period of twenty-five years.[17]

Skeptics will say that men and women who seek out college opportunities while incarcerated are a special self-selected group made up of individuals who are less likely to recidivate even if they did not go to college. While that may be true, there is strong evidence that going to college helps people realize their desire to avoid a return to prison by enabling them to land good jobs and otherwise reintegrate successfully into their families and communities.

The potential national savings from lowered costs of incarceration are substantial. Those costs have become an increasingly heavy burden due to the dramatic increase in the last several decades in the number of people in American prisons. The U.S. prison population is by far the largest in the world, both in absolute numbers and as a proportion of the total population. According to the U.S. Department of Justice, the country imprisoned 2.2 million people in 2014, and the total number of people under the supervision of the justice system—those on probation, parole, or other types of supervision—was almost 6.9 million that year.[18] By contrast, China, the world's largest country, with an estimated population of 1.3 billion, which is more than four times that of the United States, reportedly imprisons many fewer of its citizens. According to one of the best recent estimates, China ranks second in the world, with a prison population of 1.65 million (no good numbers are available for those in other kinds of detention or supervision). Proportionately, that means that in the United States, considering just those in prison, the total comes to 698 people per 100,000, whereas in China it amounts to 119 per 100,000. The magnitude of the U.S. number becomes even clearer when compared to the average number of people incarcerated in Western European countries, which is 84 per 100,000.[19]

Since the early 1970s, the prison population has spiked at an unprecedented rate, with the combined state and federal counts growing sevenfold by 2003.[20] A study conducted four years later, in 2007, showed that one in thirty men aged twenty to thirty-four was behind bars, with the proportion rising to one in nine for African American males that age.[21] Incarceration rates peaked in 2009 and 2010 and then declined slightly. However, the prison population grew again in 2014, and estimates suggest that the overall state prison population will have grown by another 3 percent by 2018.[22]

Because many more people are incarcerated in state facilities than in federal institutions, the states bear the lion's share of the costs. In 2014, while facilities under federal management housed 210,567 inmates, the number housed by the states was 1,350,958.[23] One calculation of the average annual expense for each federal inmate in 2014 put the number at $30,619.85, which amounts to an estimated total of well over $6.5 billion just for direct incarceration costs.[24] The figures for state expenses vary greatly from state to state, in part because the number of people held varies so much and in part because the average cost of housing them differs greatly. A study released in 2012 by the Vera Institute of Justice offers the best available total of state costs. The Vera researchers sent a survey to all fifty state governments asking for the data for their expenses associated with imprisonment. Only forty states responded, so the study's numbers are not national totals. But the costs for the forty states that did respond amounted to approximately $38.9 billion, a staggering number, and these costs have escalated considerably, with one calculation being that between 1987 and 2007 the expense across all states increased 127 percent.[25]

Some recent research has projected the potential savings that might be generated by reducing recidivism. The Pew Charitable Trusts conducted a study in which forty-one states participated, calculating that for a 10 percent reduction in recidivism—which is well within the bounds of the rates of reduction reported for a wide range of advanced education programs in prisons—the total savings would be $635 million in one year alone.[26] Impressive as that number is, it does not actually capture the full savings from direct costs to the states. That is because research has shown that many of the costs associated with running prisons are not adequately represented in states' budget accounts. The Vera researchers determined that most of the forty states in their study did not include the following big-ticket items in their budgets for corrections:

- Full funding for retiree health care (underfunded by $1.9 billion)
- Employee benefits, especially health care (underfunded by $613 million)
- State contributions to pensions for corrections department employees (underfunded by $598 million)
- Capital costs ($486 million not included in the corrections budget)
- Hospital and other health costs for prison population ($335 million not included)

In all, the researchers calculated, the price of prisons to taxpayers was $5.4 billion more than the sum of the forty states' corrections budgets.[27]

When considering the economic burden of prison costs, it is also important to note that many of those costs are expected to rise in the foreseeable future. For example, as prison populations age, health costs will likely increase. Between 1999 and 2013, the number of people aged fifty-five or older in state or federal prisons increased 234 percent, from 43,300 to 144,500. During the same period, the prison population that was younger than fifty-five grew much more slowly: up 9 percent, from 1.26 million to 1.37 million.[28] According to a report issued by the American Civil Liberties Union in 2012, nearly a quarter of a million men and women in state and federal prisons—enough to fill the Rose Bowl nearly three times—are classified as "elderly" or "aging."[29] That designation applies to people aged fifty and older whose aging process, according to the National Institute of Corrections, is often accelerated by general poor health before entering prison and the stress of confinement once there.[30]

As the number of people who have grown old behind bars has increased, so has the cost of providing them with health care. The National Institute of Corrections has reported that the annual cost of incarcerating people aged fifty-five and older with chronic and terminal illnesses is on average two to three times that for all other people in custody. The Federal Bureau of Prisons reports that the cost of housing an "average" individual was $28,893 per year in 2013, while the cost of housing someone at a federal prison medical facility was $57,962.[31]

Other expenses associated with continuing massive imprisonment are also likely to grow. A number of states expect the prison population to rise, which will possibly require them to build new prisons. For example, research commissioned by the Washington State government determined that the state will likely have to construct two new prisons by 2020 and a third by 2030. According to good estimates, each of them will cost approximately $250 million to build and another $45 million annually to operate.[32]

This same study provides strong evidence that offering more education programs in prisons would be one of the best ways to reduce the state's prison population. Part of the researchers' assignment was to evaluate the steps the state might take to bring the prison population down in order to obviate the need for the new prisons. In an exhaustive review of types of programs aimed at preventing recidivism, which included education programs as well as drug treatment, job training in the community, and several others, the researchers conclude that offering more education programs would be one of the most effective—and cost-effective—means.

Unfortunately, the report does not break out the results for lowered recidivism for those who took college-level classes: instead, college classes were combined with less advanced education, including GED classes. But it is notable that in advocating for increasing education programs as one of their key conclusions, the researchers do argue for more college offerings.

Senator Claiborne Pell, who sponsored the legislation that created Pell Grants, understood the savings that could be achieved by supporting college in prison. In 1994, while fighting to keep Pell eligibility for the incarcerated, he said on the Senate floor: "Diplomas are crime stoppers. It costs much less to educate a prisoner than it does to keep one behind bars."[33] Consider the case of Anthony Cardenales. The total cost of his college education, over seven years, was roughly $35,000, whereas the cost of what might be thought of as his room and board was more than $420,000. If he had returned to prison within two years, in 2011, as is true for the vast majority of those who are released and then returned to prison, the state would have paid roughly $60,000 a year to keep him locked up, with the total sum ballooning depending on the length of his sentence.[34]

A number of studies have demonstrated that the savings that could be realized by likely reductions in recidivism far outweigh the costs of providing college in prison. Most such studies have included the full range of education programs—college classes as well as vocational training and GED classes—so they do not allow for the calculation of a cost-to-benefit ratio specifically for college offerings. Nonetheless, the findings regarding the fuller range of education offerings are important to note. The RAND Corporation conducted the most comprehensive inquiry in 2013, commissioned by the U.S. Department of Justice. The RAND investigators compiled the findings from all studies released between 1980 and 2011 that met rigorous standards and determined that the return for each dollar invested in all of the types of education taken together was five dollars saved from reductions in the cost of prisons.[35] As returns on investment go, whether in financial investment, business, or public policy, that is impressive.

The research commissioned by Washington State also made such calculations. For the vocational education programs, the cost per student was $1,182 and for that investment the state saved $6,806; for the basic adult education and postsecondary education programs combined, the cost was $963 per student and the savings were $5,306.[36] In a study of recidivism among 3,600 people formerly in custody in Maryland, Minnesota, and Ohio, the researchers found that every dollar spent on education returned more than two dollars to the public in reduced prison costs.[37] The researchers from Baylor University who conducted the evaluation of the Prison Entrepreneurship Program in Texas also calculated costs versus returns, and they did so for each year out of the five years during which they tracked the recidivism of students. This is helpful in showing how the savings accrue over time, because the longer the students stayed out of prison, the higher the savings were. The study determined that for an outlay of $2 million to run the program annually, a return of $.74 on every $1.00 was achieved in year one, a $2.07 return in year three, and a $3.40 return in year five.[38]

Are college classes more effective in reducing recidivism than other kinds of education programs? To answer that question well, more extensive research is needed, especially given that the number of college programs is so small and some of them have not been operating for very long. But consider these numbers. The RAND study mentioned above calculated an average recidivism rate for all types of education programs of 30.4 percent. The study that tracked results in Maryland, Minnesota, and Ohio estimated a strikingly similar rate of 29 percent. The rates from these two studies are considerably higher than the single-digit rates reported by the four-year degree-granting programs mentioned earlier, which typically run about 2 percent.

Some additional research suggests, in fact, that the higher the degree earned, the lower the recidivism rate. The Texas Department of Criminal Justice conducted a study in 2000 that compared rates of recidivism by type of degree—associate's versus bachelor's—and also compared those rates to the system-wide recidivism rate of 43 percent at that time. The researchers found that the recidivism rate for those who earned an associate's degree was 27.2 percent, while for those who earned a bachelor's degree it was 7.8 percent.[39] Another study that reported a remarkably parallel result for obtaining an associate's degree supports this finding. In this case, the researchers studied a program in Texas that offered only the two-year degree. It showed an almost identical 27 percent recidivism rate for graduates.[40]

One other study reviewed all the evidence from before and after the Pell Grant cutoff, wherever possible focusing on studies that compared different types of education. The most interesting of these found that 37 percent of the people who had participated in postsecondary education while in prison were returned after release in comparison to 39 percent for those who had participated in vocational education, 41 percent for those enrolled in adult basic education or GED classes, and 43 percent for nonparticipants.[41] The researchers conclude, "Our results suggest that college has a substantially stronger negative impact upon recidivism hazard rates than do other forms of correctional education (e.g. high school, GED, vocational education)."[42]

As impressive as calculations of the potential direct savings from reduced recidivism are, they do not reflect the full economic benefits of advanced education in prison. Savings from reduced costs of crime must also be considered. The reductions seen in recidivism do not allow for a definite calculation of fewer crimes committed because some of those who do not return to prison may commit crimes, but not be apprehended for them. It is reasonable to assume, however, that a significant portion of those who do not return to prison have desisted from crime, and that leads to considerable savings in the costs of crime. They include victims' costs, which can take many different forms, from lost property to health care expenses and lost wages, along with the considerable costs associated with policing and prosecution. One of the best estimates of these costs was generated by the U.S. Department of Justice for crimes committed in 2007. It showed that in just that year more than 23 million criminal offenses were committed in this country, resulting in approximately $15 billion in economic losses to the victims and $179 billion in government expenditures on police protection, judicial and legal activities, and corrections.[43]

Some recent research has offered a thoughtful examination of the potential savings from crime reduction due to education in prison. Two researchers at the University of California at Los Angeles School of Public Policy and Social Research conducted a comparison of the potential savings in the costs of crime from education programs as opposed to incarceration without education. They reasoned that because educational attainment increases income, and increased income correlates with decreased involvement in crime, investments in education in prison should lower the crime rate among the formerly incarcerated. The findings of lowered recidivism provide strong evidence that their reasoning is valid. They then drew on the data about rearrest, reconviction, and reincarceration from the study of outcomes in Maryland, Minnesota, and Ohio mentioned above and conducted calculations that showed that the various kinds of education programs offered in prisons, all taken together, are twice as effective in preventing crime as incarceration without such programming. Their final calculations of the comparative savings showed that $1 million spent on correctional education could prevent 600 crimes, while the same money spent on imprisonment alone would prevent only 350 crimes.[44]

The recent studies of the reductions in recidivism due to education, complemented by this finding about the potential higher cost-effectiveness of education in reducing crime, underscore the need for a serious reexamination of the argument that a higher rate of incarceration itself is a cost-effective crime reducer. That argument gained support from a 1996 study conducted by economist Steven Levitt of *Freakonomics* fame. Levitt calculated that incarceration significantly reduced crime, but made no attempt to measure the comparative crime-reduction effects of education. Although he did argue that "If truly feasible, prevention or rehabilitation would likely be preferable to long-term incarceration from both a cost-benefit and humanitarian perspective," this was not the message that was taken from his work.[45] That is unfortunate. Any assessment of approaches to lowering the crime rate should now take account of evidence concerning the considerable impact and cost-effectiveness of education programs. That suggests that the country can both reduce crime more effectively and save substantial money by shifting from a preference for increasing incarceration to expanding education offerings.

Money saved by reducing recidivism could be spent in many socially beneficial ways. The funds that cover the costs of prisons come out of each state's general budget fund, which also pays for education, health care, public assistance, and housing, among other expenses. As states have faced increasingly tight budgets in recent years, as well as large shortfalls in revenues, the heavy burden of prison costs has cut directly into the money available for other priorities, including improvements in the salaries of teachers and those of municipal workers and building new public transportation systems. In fact, a 2014 report by the Center on Budget and Policy Priorities concluded that if state spending on prisons had remained at the level of the mid-1980s, adjusted for inflation, all states combined would today have $28 billion more in discretionary funds to dedicate to nonprison expenses.[46]

A particularly pernicious effect of the budget crunch many states have faced has been a reduction in spending on public education. That is true for spending on higher education and on K–12. Since the mid-1980s, while outlays for corrections in most states have increased, state investments in higher education have declined. State funding for higher education was 40.2 percent less in 2011 than in 1980.[47] Comparing spending increases for prisons in many states and decreases for higher education is alarming. For example, a 2012 study reports that California, the state with the largest public university system, spent 13 percent less of its general fund on higher education in 2011 than it had in 1980, while the proportion of the fund that went to corrections had risen 436 percent over the same time period.[48] Another report shows that between 1984 and 1994, California built twenty-one new prisons and only one new state university, and in that time, funding for the prison system increased by 209 percent, while funding for the state university system increased by only 15 percent.[49]

By 2013, in eleven states, spending for prisons had exceeded spending for higher education, with Oregon spending twice as much on prisons and Arizona spending 40 percent more.[50] The imbalance in funding between prisons and education was so extreme in Arizona that when Governor Doug Ducey proposed in February 2015 that the state spend an additional $70 million per year to house people in private prisons, critics objected on the grounds that this would mean the state would be using one out of every eight dollars for prisons at the same time that Ducey was requesting a $75 million cut in state aid for universities.[51] If current trends continue, state fiscal support for higher education will reach zero by 2059.[52]

As states have faced increasing difficulty providing financial support for public colleges, a major way in which they have sought additional funds has been by raising tuition as well as charging higher fees for access to libraries and computer facilities and such ancillary services as athletics and counseling. This has placed an increasing burden on students and parents. Between 1991 and 2013, in-state tuition more than doubled at public institutions and tuition rose 43 percent for out-of-state students.[53]

Add in one more factor and the perfect storm that has made higher education more expensive comes fully into view. Early in the Reagan administration, the balance between federal financial aid in the form of grants and loans shifted. Loans became the predominant vehicle by which students funded their college education. This shift contributed to mushrooming student debt. Large numbers of students have left college before finishing their degrees because they could not afford to carry any more loans.

Taken together, these developments reversed the trend toward more generous financial aid for college that began with the post–World War II GI Bill passed in 1944. Then the President's Commission on Higher Education established by Harry S. Truman in 1947 argued strongly for increased access to higher education. Known as the Truman Commission, the group maintained that "only an informed, thoughtful, tolerant people can develop and maintain a free society," which meant that in a democratic society all people, regardless of their race, religion, sex, or future occupation, should have access to the kind of general education colleges provide.[54] This encouraged a transition from elite to mass higher education and helped pave the way for colleges and universities to become more diverse in type, including the creation of more community colleges in state systems of higher education, and enrolling larger and more socially encompassing student bodies. American higher education also came to support more multifaceted faculty roles and to broaden its curriculum. As all this occurred over the following twenty years, increasing federal aid enabled more institutions of

higher education to enroll many more qualified high school graduates regardless of their capacity to pay fees or tuition. To paraphrase
the apt title of the classic sociological study of open admission at
the City University of New York, going to college came to be seen
by more Americans as a "right" rather than a "privilege."[55]

More recently, of course, as state investments in higher education have declined, partly as a result of funds being used for prisons, going to college has become prohibitively expensive for many
who would like to attend. The desire to attend college is high, despite the costs, but too many people cannot afford to enroll or to
finish their degrees. That is a travesty. Not going to college limits
one's career prospects and holds down earnings. A study released in
2010 shows a worrisome wage gap between high school and college
graduates of 83 percent.[56] In addition, as Anthony Carnevale and
his colleagues at the Georgetown University Center on Education
and the Workforce have demonstrated, the country needs more
college graduates. All these factors—the historic commitment to
increasing access, economic demand, and growing costs—have
stimulated a variety of plans to make "college for all" a reality. The
goal of such plans is to make at least the first two years of college as
widely and freely accessible as high school is today. That is clearly
in the best interest of everyone, and offering college programs in
prisons must be part of the college-for-all initiatives beginning to
develop across the nation.

Of course, empowering more people to attend and graduate from
college begins with their precollegiate schooling, and here as well,
the drain of funds from state budgets due to increased prison costs
has hit hard. In 2010, thirty-three of fifty states saw an increased
percentage of their general funds going to corrections accompanied
by a decrease in spending not only for higher education but also
for K–12 schools.[57] For example, in 2007, the federal government
spent $37 billion on "justice-related expenditures" and $14 billion
on Title I grants to school districts, which represents the largest

federal investment in K–12 education.[58] Funds for primary schools
took an additional hit from the recession beginning in 2008, and
in many states they have not rebounded fully. At least thirty states
set their per-pupil funding for K–12 schooling for 2014 at rates that
were lower than those in place before the recession.[59]

Prisons diminish human capital. Investments in education increase it. More informed debate about the costs of incarceration
is likely to foster agreement that recent funding trends must be
reversed, with investments in education restored and protected.
Mindful of negative tradeoffs between prisons and public schools,
a number of governors from both political parties have argued
powerfully that prison spending must be trimmed and education
spending boosted. Former Michigan governor Jennifer Granholm,
who is a Democrat, made the case that "it's not good public policy"
to invest in the prison system when we need to be investing "in
the things that are going to transform the economy, including education and diversifying the economy."[60] Former California governor
Arnold Schwarzenegger, a Republican, made the point even more
forcefully in 2010, by which time his state was spending 45 percent
more on prisons than universities. "Closing universities over prisons," he asserted, "is a historic and transforming realignment for
California's priorities. What does it say about any state that focuses
more on prison uniforms than on caps and gowns?" He argued for
more investment in rehabilitation and education throughout the
California correctional system as a way to rein in costs.[61]

Offering more opportunities for advanced education in prisons is
by no means the only way to cut returns to prison, nor is it the most
direct way to cut overall prison populations. In addressing the consequences of the policies and practices that have resulted in such
massive imprisonment in the United States, it is important to consider multiple strategies, over many years. Sentencing reforms are
crucial. So are changes in drug laws, especially those pertaining to

crack cocaine and marijuana. Alternatives to incarceration, such as community sentencing, need to be widely tried and evaluated. But college in prison is known to be the best means available to help people already in prison return to society ready and able to secure and hold good, family-wage jobs. College in prison is a proven investment in both personal well-being and the public good.

It is also important to note that, to be most effective, an increase in college programs must be coupled with policies to encourage job creation. The neighborhoods to which many formerly incarcerated men and women return offer scant prospects for employment. It is also the case that good jobs are in too short supply all over the country. A particular problem is that the public-sector jobs that have been so important in increasing employment in the past, particularly for African Americans, have dwindled in number. Structural economic conditions such as these must be more effectively addressed if the potential economic value of college in prison is to be fully realized.[62]

Optimizing the potential of college in prison also requires that many other needs of formerly incarcerated men and women are addressed as they move back into life on the outside. Finding suitable housing as well as health care is especially critical, and some college programs are helping with that through referrals to appropriate agencies. In many cases, men and women who have begun college degrees in prison run into obstacles as they try to continue work toward degrees after they go home. That is especially the case at institutions that continue to ask applicants if they have a criminal record. Many formerly incarcerated students need assistance not only in negotiating the admission process but also in filling out financial aid applications and arranging to transfer credits. Bard and some other college programs provide help with all this, as do special organizations such as the College and Community Fellowship led by Vivian Nixon, herself a formerly incarcerated individual who was queried about her record when she first applied to college. More such support programs are needed, and creating them should be a priority for both public and private organizations.

Education is not a panacea. But it is an extremely powerful way to intervene in the trajectory of individual lives and to support economic, social, and civic development. We need more people leaving prison the way Anthony Cardenales did. His story demonstrates that college in prison is a smart economic investment that advances the American tradition of relying on education to help individuals get ahead, while fostering both a growing economy and a vibrant democracy.

3

Instilling Purpose, Curbing Violence

The Impact of College on Life in Prison

Norma Stafford grew up on a farm in the hill country of Tennessee in a poor family with ten children. She was the only one of the ten to graduate from high school. As a lesbian, she suffered discrimination, and after trying to find acceptance by marrying a man, she left home, traveling around the country forging checks. That resulted in five years in prison, first in Alabama, and then in California. As Stafford explains in an essay for the book *13 Women: Parables from Prison*, the strict routine of life in prison combined with the lack of purposeful activities undermined her sense of self. "I functioned only when a guard pulled a lever," she writes. "When they pushed another lever, I would stand, sit, eat or lie down and sleep. . . . I succumbed to mental lethargy, and physical lethargy overwhelmed me." In prison, Stafford also began to lose any sense that life had meaning. "For almost a year I just drifted through my time," she writes. "At night, alone in my cell, I saw myself as a robot." But then she took a women's studies course that was offered by the Santa Cruz Women's Prison Project as part of a four-year program, and she began to come alive. "Never before had a college or university been here," she writes. "They brought us books. . . . Dear God! What excitement, what energy flowed through those classes." As Norma explains, "It was in this class where I discovered I could write something other than bad checks."

When the prison administration decided to cancel the program, she led a protest, and the classes were reinstated. She began to write poetry, and after she was released some of her poems were published in periodicals and she started giving readings, even doing guest lectures at a number of universities around the country. She also began speaking at events to raise money to support college-in-prison programs.[1]

Norma Stafford's story demonstrates how important college programs are in helping men and women in prison cope with the dehumanizing experience of living behind bars and emerge ready to embrace new possibilities for their lives. The alternative is simply to languish, feeling beaten down, or, for some, to be further schooled in crime. College programs also have a far-reaching, positive impact on the quality of life within a prison, improving a prison's overall atmosphere. To understand why having college programs has this effect, it is important to consider what people who live and work in prisons, as well as those who study the prison experience, say about life on the inside. Depictions in popular culture, whether in the movies or on TV, tend either to focus on the violence in prisons, often sensationalizing it, or to depict prisons as more amenable places than many actually are.

By all accounts, life inside American prisons is tough—tough on the men and women mandated to live there as well as on the people who supervise them. While the threat of violence is one aspect of this, what is less commonly understood is how stultifying time in prison is, how it saps people of a sense of purpose and undermines their sense of agency over their lives. This is partly due to their separation from family and friends and from so many features of "normal" life, and partly due to the strict regulation of their lives and lack of meaningful pursuits.

When people are transported to prison, they enter an alien world that distances them from society and the norms of life on the outside not only physically but also psychically. For many of the incarcerated, visits and calls from family members are infrequent; some have no visitors at all. Despite being forced to live in such close quarters with so many other men or women, many of those who have written about life in prison emphasize the isolation of the experience. "When I'm asked about what prison is like," one incarcerated man writes in an article entitled "A Day in the Life of a Prisoner," "I offer that it is an extremely lonely place."[2]

Strict rules govern virtually every aspect of life, from when to shower and eat to when to sleep and wake, and corrections officers are officially required to conduct close surveillance of adherence to the rules, issuing disciplinary "tickets" to those who commit infractions. Whether living in a cell in a long cell block or in dormitory-style housing, people in prisons have little to no privacy, and individuals are allowed no input into who shares their living space. Daily routines in prisons vary little: breakfast is early, usually around 6 a.m., lunch is generally at eleven, and dinner is served at five. Menus in the mess hall may change somewhat across the seasons, but typically they feature a limited rotation of dishes, with stew for dinner on Monday, ravioli on Tuesday, corn dogs on Wednesday. At regular intervals, all those in custody must return to their cells for "the count," which typically takes about thirty minutes. Lights-out is generally around midnight. Criminologist John Irwin, who specialized in the study of the American prison system, wrote in his book *The Warehouse Prison* (2005) that because their lives are so routinized and strictly regulated, men and women in prison eventually lose their "capacity to . . . control their destiny."[3] He quotes one man who wrote about the effects of this extreme control and the monotony of prison life:

In my world, every day is the same, Saturdays are like Mondays,
    and Tuesdays are like Sundays, there is no difference. . . .

In my world, my life is lived on a basis of commands. Decisions
are made, not by me, but by those who are in control. . . .
In my world, boredom is the killer.[4]

In his book *In the Place of Justice*, Wilbert Rideau vividly describes
the sense of alienation from society and psychological strain of the
tedium of confinement. Having served a long sentence in Louisiana's Angola prison, he recounts his thoughts during one of many
nights pacing his cell this way:

It's hard to believe that I once experienced a life in the world
outside my window. Would I even be able to recognize the
neighborhood I grew up in? Are kids playing hooky still
shooting craps on those old tombs? Is Old Man Martello still
peddling cigarettes three for a nickel to underage smokers? I
wonder, but there's no one to ask. Everyone but my mother has
abandoned me.

I turn from the window and walk slowly toward the heavy
steel door. I'm restless again. One . . . two . . . three . . .
four . . . five . . . turn. Walk back. One . . . two . . . three . . .
four . . . five . . . stop.[5]

Although it is important to bear in mind that prisons vary widely,
many are simply "warehousing" the men and women they hold in
custody. They provide only limited work opportunities, with much
of the work being menial labor in the laundry, food services, or general custodial support, and little more than the bare basics of literacy education and GED classes. Such prisons are focused primarily
on incapacitation, aiming to contain the incarcerated to prevent
further crime, and on punishment, rather than on any significant
efforts to help them develop the skills and perspectives that will
enhance a successful return to society as law-abiding, productive
members of communities. The tough-on-crime view that has been

so popular in recent decades has supported this approach, insisting that prisons should be institutions of confinement and retribution and not of education and rehabilitation.

People who have been to prison often state that the lack of meaningful activity not only increases the loneliness and experience of isolation, but also adds to the sense of worthlessness that separation from significant others can cause. The bars and concertina wire are always there to remind people in prison of their inability to connect. If a family member is sick, for example, they may not be able to get word about how they are doing. If a grandparent or parent dies, they may not be able to go to the funeral. If a sibling or a child is looking for work, they can do little to help. If a spouse decides it's time to split, they can do little to convince him or her otherwise. As prolific prison writer Jon Marc Taylor declares, "In prison one is immersed in continual reminders of one's 'worthlessness.'"[6]

With so little to do, many people in prison spend a great deal of time watching TV. In some prisons, televisions are made available in each cell to encourage men to remain inside their cells or dormitories rather than going out to the yard, where trouble often begins. In his book *Going up the River*, prizewinning journalist Joseph T. Hallinan reports on his investigation into the conditions at a number of prisons around the country. He quotes a prison superintendent he interviewed explaining that TV "acts like 'electronic Thorazine.' It keeps people tranquil."[7] An op-ed in the *New York Times* written by a man in custody at Attica prison in upstate New York, where the famous 1971 riot occurred and which continues to have a reputation as an exceptionally violent place, indicates that people in prison are well aware of the rationale for so much TV. He says, "We don't have access to the Internet but prison officials are all for TVs in the cells. It's called the 'TV Program.' We're entertained and confined and everyone's happy."[8] Former prisoner Michael G. Santos writes of the psychological impact of this "warehousing" with so few opportunities for growth and development, "As soon as gates lock a man inside, the prisoner learns that the goal of the corrections system is to store his body until his sentence expires. With little encouragement to grow and develop, hope for the future is easily lost."[9]

Many people who have been to prison have written about the way the experience drained their life of meaning. "For me, and many like me in prison," one man has observed, "violence is not the major problem; the major problem is monotony. It is the dull sameness of prison life, its idleness and boredom, that grinds me down. Nothing matters; everything is inconsequential other than when you will be free and how to make time pass until then."[10] Life in prison is said to feel endless. *New Yorker* writer Adam Gopnik writes evocatively in an essay entitled "The Caging of America," that "No one who has been inside a prison, if only for a day, can ever forget the feeling. Time stops."[11] Men or women in solitary confinement face what one writer refers to as "crippling monotony."[12] For corrections officers, too, the routine can be numbing. Journalist Ted Conover, who worked for a year as a corrections officer at Sing Sing in order to write about the life of officers, observes in his book *Newjack* that "prison work was about waiting. The inmates waited for their sentences to run out, and the officers waited for retirement." Quoting an officer he got to know, he maintains that being a corrections officer is " 'a life sentence in eight hour shifts.' "[13]

In *The Society of Captives*, a classic of prison research, criminologist Gresham M. Sykes emphasizes that the psychological strains of prison life can be every bit as damaging as physical assaults, if not more so. Referring to the "pains of deprivation" caused by being cut off from so many aspects of the world, he says, "However painful these frustrations or deprivations may be in the immediate terms of thwarted goals, discomfort, boredom, and loneliness, they carry a more profound hurt as a set of threats or attacks which are directed against the very foundations of the prisoner's being, the individual's picture of himself as a person of value."[14]

The challenge to an individual's sense of self can be so powerful that some among the incarcerated go through a process of "prisonization," coping with the loneliness and degradation by internalizing the mores and cultural expectations of life in prison.[15] Michael Morton was wrongfully convicted in 1987 of killing his wife and spent twenty-five years in prison before being exonerated. "Part of me adapted to prison," he later recounted, "while part of me tried to hang on to the person I used to be. I fought the insidious creep of prison slang and mannerisms into my personality. I struggled against the crudeness that comes from living in state-sanctioned internal exile. . . . But despite everything I tried and all the good intentions in the world, prison wore me down."[16] Christopher Zoukis, who went to prison for eight years beginning when he was twenty, writes, "The years grinded on. The people always the same, the disrespect and dismissal from fellow inmates and prison guards alike taking their toll incident by incident. The whole time my fear of who I might become nagging at my subconscious. . . . I was becoming what I hated in those around me."[17] Michael Santos has written thoughtfully about what he calls the "life inside mentality." "The more time I spent in the penitentiary," he recalls, "the more I came to believe that it is truly a culture unto itself . . . a culture that perpetuates failure. . . . The penitentiary discourages the men it contains from thinking they can be anything more than prisoners."[18]

From many accounts and interviews with those who have been incarcerated as well as with corrections professionals, it is clear that being able to participate in higher education is a great aid in coping with these psychological stresses of prison life. Santos is one of those who says that going to college helped him maintain a sense of hope for his future. His prospects had looked dim—he had been sentenced in 1987 to forty-five years for drug dealing.

But while serving that sentence, he was able to earn an undergraduate degree from Mercer University well as a master's degree from Hofstra University. He served twenty-six years and now works as a consultant and lawyer helping prisoners with legal matters and reentry into society after release. Remembering a debate between students in the Bard Prison Initiative and the West Point debate team, one former Bard student recalls having been approached by visitors and asked if he had thought about becoming a lawyer. Describing this later, he explained, "I had forgotten I was more than a prisoner. I had accepted the idea that I really was a bum, and the visitors' comments reminded me that I had to resist giving in to the way I was seen in there."[19] Jon Marc Taylor says this about going to college in prison: "An oasis of hope must be discovered if sanity is to prevail. For me as well as thousands of others, that refuge has been the Shangri-La of college and university extension programs in the prisons."[20] One woman who went to college while at Bedford Hills told the researchers who studied the college program there, "You can ignore all that bad stuff during the day if you know at six o'clock p.m., you're going to class."[21]

The intellectual challenge and excitement of learning not only counteract boredom; going to college helps to instill a sense of purpose and ambition for the future. Being treated as a student, as a person who is worthy of a professor's time and who has meaningful insights to offer, also helps to build self-esteem, as does discovering that one can master the rigorous assignments and do well on papers and tests. One student recalled how important it was to him that in attending college while in prison "I was fully a student, not an inmate." When asked why the experience had been so powerful for him, he responded, "It's the confidence. The confidence we get is what makes us feel like Giants. We become human and students in a world/environment that generally regards us as otherwise in so many ways, subtle and explicit."[22]

Course work provides connections to life on the outside, whether through reading history, discussing current events, or learning about other cultures or new scientific discoveries. The interaction with faculty members and student tutors from a college's main campus is also stressed by incarcerated students for the help it provides in combating feelings of separation from normal life and the loneliness many in prison feel. According to a wide range of men and women who have gone to college while in prison, the experience of having a community of peers, joined by common academic goals and intellectual interests, is perhaps the most important social benefit. Students develop friendships and create networks of support, helping each other pursue their goals, both the larger goal of self-development and the smaller, more immediate goals involved in taking tough classes or studying for a difficult test or coping with an especially challenging instructor. Sean Simms, a student in the Prison University Project at San Quentin, observes, "The College Program has created such a positive, energetic environment that is completely separate from the rest of the prison. . . . I now have a new sense of community. I am able to broaden my base of friends and enjoy speaking about school work with fellow classmates that I never would have been able to associate with."[23]

It must be said that not all facilities are devoid of purposeful activities. Prisons vary a great deal, and of the roughly five thousand adult jails and prisons in the United States, no two are fully alike.[24] They differ, for one thing, in terms of security levels, from minimum-security facilities to medium security, maximum security, and supermax, with the lower security levels housing primarily offenders convicted of nonviolent crimes and the higher levels holding offenders convicted of violent crimes. Some prisons are massive complexes that combine several different security levels with very different conditions in each. They also vary significantly in terms of how many recreational, educational, and work facilities they offer.

Some prisons offer a wide range of vocational classes and work opportunities, some of which may be educational, but others of which may be grossly exploitive, bringing profits to the correctional authorities and the profit-making companies involved and paying the incarcerated workers only pennies an hour. There are work programs that allow participation in off-site businesses in the surrounding community for low-level, nonviolent offenders, and there are a number that operate factories, or collaborate with private interests in running them—the factory inside the Eastern Oregon Correctional Institution, which makes clothing for the Prison Blues brand, is one example. Still others run large farming operations, such as the one at the Angola prison in Louisiana, which was built on the site of a former slave plantation, and now requires some of the people held there to work on the farm. A number of prisons have recently created farming and gardening programs that are designed primarily for educational purposes rather than as income generators. These teach skills and help provide the prisons with fresh produce.

The widely ranging views of wardens regarding the appropriate way to run a facility have a significant impact on conditions within a prison. Some wardens take a tough, punitive approach and do not view their prisons as institutions that should offer opportunities for the men or women in custody to grow and develop in positive ways, while others are big believers in that mission. Some have participated in efforts to find ways to make prisons more humane, such as a multistate program organized by the National Institute of Corrections, called the Institutional Culture Initiative, which sought to identify interventions that could help to improve conditions.

Combating the violence that plagues many prisons is a key motivation for efforts to reform the culture of prisons, and this is another way in which providing opportunities to attend college can help to transform the experience of prison life. A study of college-in-prison programs conducted by the Correctional Association of New York, entitled *Education from the Inside Out: The Multiple Benefits of College Programs in Prison*, concludes that college programs can help to tamp down violence and have a wide-reaching positive effect on a prison's culture. Jamie Houston, director of the Correctional Education Program at Indiana State University, who also served as an assistant warden in the Indiana Department of Corrections, told the researchers that college-in-prison students are "the best-behaved population in a correctional facility."[25] Robert Cadigan, of the Boston University Prison Education Program, is quoted in the report, observing that college programs produce a "rising tide lifting all boats."[26] The report concludes that offering college programs is one effective way to make prisons safer, both for those who are incarcerated and for corrections officers. In addition, a study of the college program at the Bedford Hills Correctional Facility, the maximum-security women's prison in Westchester, New York, led by social psychologist Michelle Fine, concludes that the college program there has made the prison more "peaceful and disciplined."[27]

Though the level of violence within prisons varies, violence is a problem throughout the federal and state prison systems, and it is regularly perpetrated by corrections officers as well as by those serving time. Adam Gopnik describes viscerally how the monotony of prison is tinged with a persistent undercurrent of threat for both officers and their charges, observing that prisons are distinguished by "A note of attenuated panic, of watchful paranoia—anxiety and boredom and fear mixed into a kind of enveloping fog, covering the guards as much as the guarded."[28] Many of the accounts of those who have lived and worked in prisons describe almost daily incidents and recall the need for constant vigilance. Raymond Roe, who attended the college program run by Cornell University at Auburn prison in upstate New York, is a large and strong man and a former Marine, but he still found his initial time in prison terrifying. "I witnessed gang fighting on a daily basis," he recalls. "I witnessed physical and mental abuse by the staff responsible for our well-being. I never was in any fights, but was in many situations where I had to confront aggressors."[29] Though women's prisons are reportedly somewhat less violent than men's facilities, they are by no means immune to problems. Amme Voz, who wrote about her prison experience in *The Nation*, states that "every day was a battle to live." On two occasions she "was sexually bullied and physically attacked." She wrote that within the prison where she was held a woman would be moved to a new facility, with a higher level of security, if she reported abuse. If a woman was threatened or attacked by corrections officers and reported the incident, she would be put in solitary. On one occasion, when Voz alleged that a corrections officer was harassing her, she was put on suicide watch, which can simply mean being monitored constantly or, in a more extreme form, having everything removed from one's cell including clothing. "No one can survive" time in prison, she believes, "without internalizing the daily subjugation of dehumanizing treatment."[30]

Accounts by those who have worked as corrections officers attest to the pervasive sense of threat as well. Ted Conover, the author of *Newjack*, noted the constant undercurrent of tension between COs and inmates. "The starting point in prison . . . was stress," he says of his first days on the job, describing the prison as "a world of adrenaline and aggression to us new officers. It was an experience of living with fear."[31]

Many factors contribute to violence in prisons, and the insights of professionals in corrections as well as scholars who study prison violence help to explain why college programs can play a mitigating role. The report of the Commission on Safety and Abuse in America's Prisons, convened in 2005 to investigate the frequency and causes of prison abuse and what could be done to improve conditions, is the most comprehensive and reliable source on this. Comprised of leading lawyers, doctors, and civil rights activists, as well as leaders in law enforcement and criminal justice, some of whom had been incarcerated, the commission was mobilized by two advocates of reform, Chris Stone, then director of the Vera Institute, and Aryeh Neier, then president of the Open Society Foundations. They were responding to the scandal provoked by the disturbing photographs taken of prisoners being abused and reports of torture at the Abu Ghraib prison in Iraq. Their hope was that the scandal would encourage attention to conditions in American prisons, where the Abu Ghraib guards had been trained. Over the course of a year, the commission held hearings across the country, took testimony from a wide range of experts, and solicited letters and emails from thousands of ordinary citizens, some of whom had family members in prison, as well as from some individuals then serving time.

The commission's report, entitled *Confronting Confinement*, describes a disturbingly high incidence of assaults—of inmates on other inmates, of inmates on corrections officers, and of corrections officers on inmates—and attributes the problem largely to the stressful, highly punitive, and unhygienic conditions found at many prisons. There are failing prisons and jails across this country, the report maintains, where discipline may be arbitrary and severe, and assaults, rapes, and beatings occur regularly.[32] The use of solitary confinement, which is widely regarded by psychologists who have studied its effects as inhumane, is also a common disciplinary practice. At the newer supermax style of facility, individuals are confined in cells for twenty-three hours a day, often for years, and the commission found that "In some places, the environment is so severe that people end up completely isolated, confined in constantly bright or constantly dim spaces without any meaningful human contact."[33]

In many other facilities, living conditions are unacceptable due to severe overcrowding and to old, poorly maintained exercise yards and cells sometimes no bigger than a king-size bed. Health care is poor, with mental health services being either nonexistent or inferior. The commission determined that overcrowding has become a major problem in many places. In 2014, the prison systems of seventeen states housed more people than they were designed to hold, sometimes far more. According to a 2012 report about federal prisons, they, too, are over capacity, by 39 percent.[34] This results in very crowded living quarters in some prisons as well as fewer opportunities for education, drug treatment, and work. It also decreases the ratio of corrections officers to the incarcerated population. The Government Accounting Office's director of homeland security echoed the commission's concerns, saying of the overcrowding: "If you start cramming more and more people into a confined space, you're going to create more tensions and problems [and] someone's going to snap and have a violent incident."[35]

Gangs have contributed significantly to prison violence. They have apparently flourished in part because they can offer members protection and in part because they fill a need for "governance" outside the sphere of official officer oversight. David Skarbek, a British scholar who has done extensive research into gangs in American prisons, has published one of the best recent analyses. He maintains that gangs emerged inside prisons to enforce norms of behavior and regulate the exchange of goods and services not sanctioned by prison authorities, especially drugs. They formed in response to the massive growth of the prison population, he argues, because that growth undermined self-imposed informal codes of conduct that had previously regulated most interaction.[36] The breakdown of codes of conduct points to another cause of violence generally, and this perspective suggests that the influence of gangs, which varies considerably among prisons and across regions, will be reduced only when prison authorities improve conditions of confinement.

Tension between corrections officers and those they supervise is identified as a major source of trouble. The *Confronting Confinement* report concludes that an "us versus them" mentality endangers both people in custody and the staff overseeing them. This tension is exacerbated, it points out, by differences in race, class, and life experience, explaining that some of the people responsible for supervision have too little understanding of the people they are asked to oversee.[37] Tension is also stoked by the fact that COs supervise all of the movements of the incarcerated, opening cells when it is time for meals and work or recreational time, ensuring that all of those on a cell block are back in their cells several times a day ready to be counted, and regularly performing searches of cells and the prison facilities for weapons and contraband. They are also the front-line enforcers of elaborate rules governing life within cell blocks, including prohibitions about clothing or towels being hung on bars or playing music too loudly. The work is fraught with opportunities for confrontation.

Ted Conover describes a battle of wills between officers and inmates that fuels attacks, both by those confined and by COs, explaining that inside the prison, "unlike in the outside world, power and authority were at stake in nearly every transaction."[38] He witnessed both exemplary supervision by COs, who showed admirable restraint in the face of infractions and taunts by inmates, as well as inappropriate behavior when officers were physically or verbally abusive or held dehumanizing views of those in their charge. One CO told him, "You are a zookeeper now. Go run the zoo."[39]

The vicious cycle of violence that mutual hostility can provoke was detailed by Keith R. Lansdowne, one of the students in a fiction writing class taught by novelist Robert Ellis Gordon in a Washington State prison. In an essay included in the edited collection *The Funhouse Mirror: Reflections on Prison*, Lansdowne recounts that after he was discovered with a homemade shank during a search at the Washington State Penitentiary in Walla Walla, he was sent to the Intensive Management Unit, or the "hole," as solitary confinement is often called. There, he recalled, "the guards rarely missed an opportunity to taunt" him. The rage this brought out in him caused him to strike out, which only got him more time in solitary.[40]

Offering more opportunities to attend college in prison would help to reduce the sources of tension and would empower more of the men and women in prison to overcome the frustrations and stay clear of the influences that can lead to violence. The *Confronting Confinement* report echoes the findings of the Correctional Association of New York cited earlier in arguing that college in prison helps to combat the behavior that leads to violence. "Education—particularly at the college level . . . reduces rule-breaking and disorder in prison," the commission concludes.[41] A wide range of additional research, much of it based on interviews with prison officials and those who have been through college-in-prison programs, further supports the positive impact education can have.

Many college-in-prison students have also stated that the presence of a college program had a positive effect throughout the facilities in which they were held. Raymond Roe, who took classes offered by Cornell at Auburn prison, asserts that there was a major change when Cornell faculty began teaching there. Aly Tamboura, serving a fifteen-year sentence in California, is eloquent in his praise for the Prison University Project at San Quentin and the powerful positive effect it has had on life generally at the prison. "The first years of my incarceration were spent at a terribly violent prison devoid of anything positive," he has stated. "For me, it was a place where hope dwindled and depression and helplessness took hold." But then he was admitted to the Prison University Project and transferred to San Quentin to enroll. "Taking college classes has transformed my existence," he explains, "from wallowing in despair and idleness to one of hope and enlightenment. As I walk the grounds of San Quentin, I see that it is not only me the college has affected; it is every man who participates in the program. The transformative power of education has changed this prison into a college campus where men are spending their time learning instead of being engaged in hostility."[42]

One reason for this effect is the boost to self-esteem that going to college provides. James Gilligan, the New York University professor and psychiatrist, emphasizes the link between self-esteem and violence in arguing that education is the best way to combat the violence problem in prisons. He explains that people who engage in violent acts do so primarily because they feel people have shamed them. He further points out that "education is one of the most powerful tools for acquiring self-esteem," and argues that "since self-esteem is the most powerful psychological force that prevents violence," education inside prisons lessens violence.[43]

The networks of friendship and support that a college program helps to foster are also instrumental in the positive influence colleges can have throughout a prison. Students who are part of a community focused on constructive goals are better able than their noncollege peers to resist the pull of prison norms and distance themselves from gang ties or from acquaintances from their prior lives in the streets. Winthrop Wetherbee, of the Cornell program, has written about this process among his students. In the yard, he explains, "social groupings are determined largely by race, [and] status, [which] often depends on the nature of your crime (murderers rule, sexual offenders are fair game) and survival may require affiliation with a gang, and the consequent obligation to prove your manhood, risking serious injury and the extension of your sentence by engaging in violence." It is enormously difficult for a man to free himself from the expectations of the yard, he maintains, but education can help. It can literally be "a life-saver."[44]

The change in atmosphere that a college program can create seems to extend beyond the circle of those who are actually enrolled. A formerly incarcerated math major who earned a bachelor's degree while in prison asserts that even a relatively small college program may have a multiplier effect across a correctional facility.

"Every student knows ten guys who are not enrolled," he explains. "That student shares class discussions and even books with those guys. One hundred students go to college and one thousand people are involved in education."[45]

Students often express their sense of community by assisting others in pursuing their education. "While at Elkhart (Indiana) County Correctional Center," a student in the Notre Dame–Holy Cross college-in-prison program has reported, "I began helping offenders with the GED classes. I also enrolled in every class . . . the jail had to offer. Other inmates saw how happy I was going to classes and they began to enroll too. Our pod soon became a place where men could build up their self-esteem and experience personal growth. I like to think I fostered and encouraged this participation."[46] Wesley Caines, the Bard alum, had a similar experience in the facilities in which he lived during the slightly more than twenty-four years (of a twenty-five-year sentence) he spent in prison. He says he tried to set an example of the discipline and self-possession one could acquire through study, and that other men who saw how much he enjoyed debating ideas chose to follow his example by participating in whatever educational activities they could find.[47]

Investigators from the Urban Institute who studied the impact of postsecondary education in four different prisons in three states (Indiana, Massachusetts, and New Mexico) found powerful support for this view. They concluded that people who had participated in postsecondary education had formed "supportive associations" with other students and were now motivated to avoid conflicts. Some of the male participants explained that graduating or just being able to stay in college became more important to them than defending themselves or joining prison disputes. For some college students, the experience apparently even "overshadowed the fact that they were incarcerated and kept them from thinking about 'doing time.'"[48]

The ability to cope better with the difficulties of prison life, and to avoid violent incidents or other infractions, is also the result of the personal growth that going to college helps to bring about. College classes can give students the knowledge and perspective they need to reexamine all that led them to prison, both their own behavior and the social circumstances of their prior lives. People who teach in college-in-prison programs often observe slowly evolving but profound changes in their students. Social scientists who have studied desistance from crime have also remarked that this is a process, not an event, and usually unfolds slowly.[49] By redefining who is and is not a peer, college can enhance the likelihood that people in prison will choose to reinvent themselves. People who have witnessed personal transformations in prison would agree with the Cornell professor who believes education can be the place where new selves are found.[50]

Many students have described how this occurred for them. Jon Marc Taylor wrote an essay about how going to college enabled him to grow intellectually as well as personally. By listening to and coming to respect the other students in his classes, his mind was opened. In particular he credits the effect of learning about the life experiences of a fellow student, named Rodney, whom he describes as "a second-generation urban gang leader [with] the intense rage of a radicalized black man." Taylor says Rodney helped him to recognize the humanity in all people, even those society would label "volatile and extremely dangerous," and that coming to understand Rodney better also helped him come to understand himself.[51] Vincent T. Greco is another college graduate who has described a personal transformation. He was sentenced to life in prison in Maryland in 1982 for rape and murder. Pell Grants were then available to people in prison, and Greco used one to help pay for studies leading to a bachelor's degree from Coppin State University. He says going to college gave him "the intellectual freedom to evaluate the emotional and other things that were going on that led to what I did." Echoing what others have also asserted, he says, "It really gave a sense of self-worth, that you're able to obtain a college degree."[52] A woman in the college program at Bedford Hills told researchers, "When I first came to Bedford Hills, I was a chronic disciplinary problem, getting tickets back to back. I had a very poor attitude as well, I was rude and obnoxious for no reason, [and] I did not care about anything or anyone. Then I became motivated to participate in a number of programs, one of which was college. I started to care about getting in trouble and became conscious of the attitudes I had that influenced my negative behavior."[53]

The changes in perspective, increasing self-respect, and growing sense of personal efficacy that succeeding in college can provide inspire many students with strong feelings of hope and determination that they can return home to their families and embark on successful careers. The Urban Institute researchers reported frequent comments to this effect by students enrolled in college programs. These students said their college experience had boosted their self-esteem because they had learned that "they could complete something," could "focus and set goals," and were "more intelligent than they had previously believed." Many participants were also proud to be the first people in their families to go to college and explained that they expected to return home "more accomplished and [better] able to establish credibility after previous mistakes." Thanks to going to college, they hoped to avoid "menial labor" and to serve as "a good example in the community." They also expressed confidence that having gone to college would ensure they did not return to prison.[54]

Students interviewed in a review of postsecondary programs in thirty-eight prisons across five states expressed the same sentiments. Comments included:

> "People see me studying in my cell and come up and ask me questions. [They] ask me to tell them about college and the classes."

"I like to learn things. . . . It's made things a lot more exciting for me. I can see things in a new light."

"It's nice to bond with inmates going in a positive direction."

"You're exposing guys to things they never thought were possible for them, you're giving them an opportunity to show that they can still do something that isn't illegal."

"When you have people [like our professors] that care about you and about you succeeding, you are able to care for someone else. . . . When you are motivated, you help motivate the next man."[55]

Across the evaluations that have been done of college-in-prison programs, the findings are consistent. Going to college enhances self-esteem and self-confidence, improves peer interactions and creates a sense of community, encourages compliance with rules and regulations, and instills hope for the future. For all of these reasons, opportunities for challenging, advanced education can help transform institutions that otherwise tend to dehumanize and diminish people into places of purposeful growth and transformation. Ensuring that people in prison are included in current efforts to develop policies that will make calls for "college for all" a reality could go a long way toward making correctional facilities more worthy of their name.

4

Families and Neighborhoods

The Spillover Effects of College in Prison

Stanley Richards exemplifies the many ways going to college in prison can have a positive impact both for the families of those who are incarcerated and for the communities from which so many of the incarcerated come, and to which they so often return after release. He is now a senior vice president at the Fortune Society and has come a long way from a troubled youth and many years spent incarcerated.

Richards grew up in the 1960s in the Soundview Houses, a public housing project in the Bronx. He started selling pot when he was thirteen and dropped out of school in ninth grade. Shortly thereafter he began using cocaine and heroin and robbing other dealers to get money to buy drugs. He was in and out of the Rikers Island jail many times, and he says he assumed the rest of his life would consist of nothing more than hanging out in the streets and cycling in and out of jail. Then he was sent to prison, where he earned a GED, passing the test on his first try. That was "a revelation," he says. It showed him that he had "the power and potential to create a life free of crime."[1] He then enrolled in a college program operated by Medaille College based in Buffalo, earning an associate's degree and finishing magna cum laude. Richards says the insight he gained inspired him to ask, "'Wait a minute, what am I doing?' . . . I am not the dumb kid who couldn't do anything, who was destined to a life of crime, prison or death, and I started realizing that the power of my life was not in the power of police officers in my community, or the system, it rested with the decisions I made."[2]

According to Richards, one of the most important outcomes of his new perspective was a stronger relationship with his family. Becoming a fully mature and productive member of society, he has said, allowed him to regain custody of his son, who had been in kinship foster care. He also got married and had four more children. He says that rebuilding family ties was critical to his continuing success. His experience forging a new life also fueled his desire to help others reunite with their families and create productive working lives after release from prison.

Criminal punishment is intended to sanction the individual who has been found guilty of a crime. But, as many commentators have noted, incarceration is often a family affair. It can affect an entire kin network, sometimes across several generations. In fact, the consequences of mass incarceration for families have been so dire that two experts on the family have written that prison policy has been "one of the most pervasive 'anti-family' policies" in the history of the United States.[3] Criminologist Todd Clear, who has studied the effects of incarceration extensively, has observed that "incarceration policy has been a fellow traveler in the deterioration of poor American families."[4]

Whole communities also suffer substantial "collateral damage." This is because incarceration is highly concentrated in neighborhoods that are devastated by poverty. Those sent to prison from these neighborhoods usually return to them when they are released, and they are often unable to find good jobs. As a consequence, the communities experience rising unemployment and with it deepening poverty and more crime. Just as incarceration has wide effects, college in prison has many positive spillover effects that help to address the problems so many families and neighborhoods face.

In order to begin examining how college-in-prison programs can help families affected by incarceration, it is important, first, to consider the problems having a family member sent to prison can cause for the relatives left behind. The harm inflicted is both direct and immediate, and indirect and longer-term.

One of the most devastating immediate effects is loss of income. Most of those who are sent to prison were contributing significantly to their family's income prior to their conviction, and most of them are parents, the vast majority being fathers. According to a 2007 estimate, roughly half of all imprisoned adults had at least one child at the time of their incarceration, and estimates indicate that some 2.7 million American children now have one or both parents in prison. That number escalated dramatically as rates of incarceration spiked in the last few decades. Twenty-five years ago, one in 125 children had a parent behind bars; today that number is one in twenty-eight (3.6 percent of all children).[5] The children of minority populations have been hit the hardest, with one in nine African American children having a parent in prison and one in twenty-eight Hispanic children, compared to one in fifty-seven white children.[6] Most of these children are young—the average age is eight years old.[7]

One study determined that over two-thirds of the men sent to prison, who account for over 93 percent of all of the incarcerated, had jobs before they were arrested and that over half of them were contributing the primary source of income for a child or children.[8] Other research has shown that two-thirds of all parents in prison were contributing to a child's financial support at the time of their conviction.[9] Even when fathers were not married to a child's mother or living with the family, most are reported to have made some cash contributions, to have bought toys or helped with household supplies, such as food and diapers, or to have provided occasional childcare services. Such contributions make a big difference in families with meager resources, helping the children, but also enabling the spouse to use scarce dollars for other purposes, perhaps overdue rent payments or electric bills or clothes for other family members.

The families from which most of the incarcerated come are poor. According to research published by the Urban Institute in 2007, about half of incarcerated parents reported a monthly income of less than $1,000 prior to arrest.[10] To help put that in perspective, the U.S. government sets the poverty line at an income of $11,770 a year for a single-member household, $15,930 for a two-member household, and $20,090 for a three-member household.[11] Clearly, many of the families of those in prison were already living in very fragile economic circumstances before a parent was sent to prison, and those circumstances are strained a good deal more thereafter.

That is due not just to the loss of income from the person in prison, but to many expenses with which the families of the incarcerated are burdened. Depending on state laws, these may include a fee per day of incarceration, which is reportedly charged in roughly half of all state prison systems, along with special charges for meals or medical and dental services. Many other required fees associated with incarceration as well as with the conditions of release include charges for police transport, electronic monitoring, and drug testing. One study, entitled *Who Pays: The True Cost of Incarceration on Families*, found that 58 percent of families could not afford these costs, which forced many into debt, with the average debt for just court-related fees and fines amounting to $13,607. That same survey found that one in five families had become unable to afford the housing they were living in due to a family member's incarceration, and that 65 percent had trouble meeting other basic needs, such as food, clothing, and transportation.[12] The spillover effects for family members can be crushing, even causing dislocation from stable housing or other traumatic changes. The *Who Pays* report quotes one formerly incarcerated person telling such a story: "Everything that was put into bailing me out was everything my mother had in savings and she borrowed some money from my grandparents. She was back to working paycheck to paycheck. Eventually, about a year and a half after being locked up, my mother had to give up the house she loved and move back to an apartment."[13] The Brennan Center for Justice reports that "an estimated 10 million people . . . owe more than $50 billion resulting from their involvement in the criminal justice system."[14] In *Doing Time on the Outside: Incarceration and Family Life in Urban America*, George Washington University law professor Donald Braman makes the point that, taken together, the lost income and financial costs of incarceration amount to "a hidden tax, one that is visited disproportionately on poor and minority families," not merely in one generation, but in the next as well.[15]

Even while serving time, people who go to college in prison can help ease their family's financial plight—albeit very modestly. College students sometimes have an advantage in getting the better paying jobs in prison. This may help a family's finances by cutting down on the amount of money family members feel they need to send in order to help pay for toiletries, food, and other items from the prison commissary while also helping to cover some of the expenses institutions levy. By far the biggest potential economic payoff for families, however, comes from the enhanced ability of those who have been to college to negotiate the difficulties of reentry to society, especially finding good jobs after release.

Returning home from prison is often a joyous event, but it comes with huge challenges as well. Restrictions imposed even after release make reentry difficult. In many states, for example, people with felony records are not eligible for food stamps and cannot reside in public housing, which can be a particular problem if that is where a family member or friend willing to take them in resides. The vast majority of people released from state prisons will spend at least several years under the supervision of a parole officer, meeting with that officer on a regular basis to report on their activities or perhaps be tested for drugs. That can be difficult, but the challenge of finding work is the highest hurdle. It can be a long, arduous, and dispiriting experience. The more difficult a time someone has with reentry, the more difficult an experience this will likely be for family members as well, who often try to assist with logistics by filling out forms, providing transportation to parole meetings, and covering expenses. A large survey of those with an incarcerated family member reported: "Family support is our national reentry program. Yet the people tasked with facilitating reentry—the families—reported little or no support, leaving them to grapple unassisted with the barriers and burdens imposed on their formerly incarcerated loved ones and themselves as family members."[16] Men and women who have been to college while in prison face all these problems, but they are much better prepared to cope with them than their noncollege peers.

The economic impact of incarceration is not limited to the period of imprisonment and the prolonged time it may take to find work; it often persists over the course of a formerly incarcerated person's entire working life. As noted earlier, research on the longer-term effects on the earnings of people who have spent time in prison reveals a "sizeable lifelong earnings gap," with the average total income earned by age forty-eight of men who had been incarcerated being between 41 percent and 50 percent lower than that of men who had not been incarcerated—and that does not include the loss of income during the period of incarceration.[17] This is a striking indicator of the continuing difficulties imposed on the families of the formerly incarcerated and how important it is that men and women who go to prison be able to earn the college credentials that can help to close the gap.

In addition to these economic benefits, going to college while in prison can help to mitigate, and even to repair, breakdowns in family relationships. Imprisonment can evoke a difficult mixture of emotions, notably anger and shame, among family members, and college can help counteract that, as well as the pain inflicted on family members by the stigmas attached to them by association.

When someone goes to prison it strains family relationships in many ways, putting great pressure on marriages and steady partner relationships as well as on parent-child bonds and those with parents and siblings. One indication of the toll taken is a finding about the incidence of divorce. Though comprehensive data about the number of divorces that follow a partner's incarceration is not available, one recent survey found that for every year a married person is in prison, the chance he or she will get divorced rises 32 percent.[18]

Geography is one reason families fall apart. Most prisons are located far away from the urban centers from which the large majority of the incarcerated come—often they are at least one hundred miles from those areas and many prisons are a good deal farther away than that. That makes visiting difficult. Long trips are both time-consuming and prohibitively expensive for many families, who often do not own cars and whose low incomes make paying for public transportation and hotel stays a heavy burden. Some people in prison see their family members rarely and some never receive visits from them at all.

Staying in touch by phone can also be difficult. Because prison policy generally prohibits incoming calls to people in custody, most calls must be collect, and the costs can be substantial. One spouse interviewed about the challenges of staying connected conveyed vividly how overwhelming that can be: "The costs of phone, food, train, lost days of work. It leaches into every aspect of your life."[19]

Another problem for families has to do with visiting procedures and conditions, which can be very unpleasant and, for children in particular, even quite scary. Due to security concerns, all visitors, even young children, are searched and required to walk through metal detectors. In some cases, prisons also restrict visitors from having any physical contact with the family member they are visiting, separating them with a glass partition and requiring them to talk by phone. Some parents or guardians do not want to expose children to these conditions. Some also do not want to cause children the emotional pain of seeing a parent as a prisoner, and some of the incarcerated do not want their children to visit because they are ashamed and do not want to be seen in such a situation.[20]

In some instances, family members may want to distance themselves from those in prison because they are angry that their son, husband, or daughter got into trouble with the law, or they may be upset about the particular crimes that sent someone away. It can also be the case that a family member is ashamed to have someone from their family imprisoned and may resent the harsh stigmatization that may be directed at them by members of their communities and the wider society. Just as the formerly incarcerated encounter prejudices in looking for housing and jobs, so their family members encounter similar prejudice when friends, neighbors, and teachers discover they have a family member "inside." "Many people do not understand what we go through as prison wives and family members," one woman explained. "People on the 'outside' don't understand our choice to enter or remain in a relationship with someone who is incarcerated, and many judge us harshly for our choices to love them and remain loyal to them. . . . [R]arely do we entrust our feelings of loss and grief at our loved one's absence with someone who doesn't even attempt to understand."[21] Sometimes family members of incarcerated people keep the fact that they have a family member in prison secret. A girl interviewed about the experience of having a father in prison recounted a common response of children with incarcerated parents who are asked about their parent's work or where their parent is, saying that she would make up a story. "It's hard to explain that to people," she commented.

"There's such a heavy stigma against people who are incarcerated or formerly incarcerated."[22]

Stigmatization is hard for people of all ages, but its effects on children are particularly troubling. Research has shown that children with a parent in prison are often denied the sympathy and social support children suffering through other difficulties such as divorce or parental death are generally offered.[23] Sometimes teachers demean them, conveying that they assume the children are like their parents and are therefore incompetent, untrustworthy, dangerous, or generally "bad." Psychologists have found that even without experiencing hostility from adults, children themselves sometimes believe their mother or father is "bad," which can lead to alienation from the parent as well as profound feelings of loneliness and low self-esteem. Todd Clear and Natasha A. Frost have reported a counterintuitive finding: stigmatization and shame are not diminished in neighborhoods in which a high proportion of parents are in prison, or have been there.[24] That may suggest the power of these shunning mechanisms as well as their potential to inflict lasting harm.

Hoping to keep word of a parent's conviction from going around, and to shield the children from harsh reactions, guardians sometimes deceive children about where their parent has gone. Children may be told that their parent has joined the military or is traveling. They cannot be given a definite answer about when the parent will return, and the continuing absence becomes increasingly mysterious and puzzling. The uncertainty about when the child may see the parent again can lead to anxiety, and children may grieve the loss. In this way, incarceration amounts to a form of "social death," which cannot be acknowledged and mourned since the person in prison is actually still alive.[25]

College-in-prison programs help to mitigate all of these adverse effects on families. Family members often become proud of their college student, admiring the commitment being made and the dedication to righting wrongs and contributing to the family's well-being after release. This can make visits and calls more positive, even inspiring, turning them into occasions that help to strengthen or even restore ties. Researchers at Bedford Hills, the maximum-security prison for women in Westchester, New York, found that the children of the college students expressed pride that their mothers were going to college. "I brag about her to all my teachers," one twelve-year-old reported. A college-in-prison student stated, "My daughter is proud of me and it gives her incentive to want to go [to college]. . . . If her mother could do it so could she." Another child happily noted, "My mother is the only person I know who went to college." Still another talked about how much she now enjoyed visiting her mother. "I know she's happy . . . I know . . . she's not happy with what the situation is, but she has an opportunity to get an education, [and] I know she's extremely pleased about that."[26]

Going to college in prison can also inspire pride in the students, and that can make them more eager for interaction with their families. One formerly incarcerated college student told researchers that he now looked forward to talking with his mother because he could fill her in about his progress in classes. "Instead of me calling [my mom] and saying, 'Nothing going on,'" he stated, "now I can call her and I can say, 'I'm reading this, I'm learning about all of these scholars' and now I can share this with my mom, and she can share that with her friends or family."[27]

College-in-prison students often report that they have gained more authority in their children's or other family members' lives, recounting conversations with a sibling or other relative about a youngster who is not doing well in school or who is engaging in risky behaviors. Because they have earned respect as college students, their admonitions carry more weight. One imprisoned father told researchers, "[My son] now takes my advice. He didn't respect my opinion [before I went to college in prison]. The way I'm talking to him has changed. He'll ask my opinion, because of the way that I'm delivering the answers."[28]

Another important way in which incarcerated students can help their family members is by inspiring them to get a good education. This is an especially important outcome for the children of incarcerated parents because running into trouble in school is one of the common ways the suffering of children with a parent in prison manifests itself. Sadly, studies show that the children of incarcerated parents are more likely to perform poorly academically and to drop out.[29] Researchers have found that the negative impact of parental incarceration is evident in lower rates of school engagement than one sees in other children, engagement being gauged by the level of a child's curiosity and interest in learning, signs of caring about how well he or she performs, and doing all the assigned homework.[30] Behavior problems are also common.[31] Fortunately, some of these problems are temporary. But others lead to long-term consequences. In a 2010 paper on the "collateral costs" of incarceration, sociologists Bruce Western and Becky Petit state that 23 percent of children with a father who had been incarcerated had been expelled or suspended from school compared to 4 percent of children with a nonincarcerated father.[32] Problems in school can, in turn, lead to long-term curtailment of life opportunities, relegating many to low-paying, nonskilled work and often to repeated or long-term unemployment.

Those who go to college while in prison can serve as positive role models for their children and other family members, exemplifying the importance of getting a good education and the need to work hard to achieve that. They can share with their children the excitement and pleasure they have found in mastering difficult material, and they can coach them about studying and not letting tough assignments, frustrations, or bad influences deter them from doing their work. College students have often commented on conversations with their children in which they compared notes about the challenge of writing well and completing homework on time. This sharing, and a parent's concern about a child's dedication to school, can be another strong force in healing relationships, both during incarceration and after release. Joe Williams, the social worker at Brooklyn Defender Services, has become deeply engaged in his daughter's life and schooling, even though she lives with her mother. He visits her school frequently—he says, "they know me there"—and he is determined that she will finish high school and go on to college and even graduate school, as he has now done.

Imprisoned college students are often the first in their family to seek a postsecondary degree, and they can inspire other family members to believe in their ability to go to college too. Indeed, college-in-prison students sometimes boast that as a result of their pursuit of a college degree, a family member is now also enrolled. The spillover effects for families may spread quite widely. One student from New York City told researchers, "I was the first one to go to school in my family, to get a college education. After that—my niece has a BA from John Jay, my nephew has a PhD and teaches at Hunter, my younger brother got his AD [associate's degree]. My mother, may she rest in peace, her thing was—'Look what you started.' And it was from the penitentiary."[33]

The strong correlation between a parent going to college and his or her children doing so is well established in education research. The *National Journal* reports that in 2013, half of all youngsters whose parents hold a bachelor's degree will earn a four-year credential, while only one-fourth of those whose parents did not earn a bachelor's will gain that credential, and among young people whose parents did not go beyond high school only one in eight will earn a four-year degree.[34] There is no research testing whether having a parent enrolled in college elevates the aspirations of their children or improves their school outcomes; incarcerated parents and their children have not been included in studies of correlations between parental and child educational attainment. Because one cannot simply presume that the results will be the same as those for other children, more research is needed. Still, the research of Michelle Fine and her associates with the families of women incarcerated at Bedford Hills as well as a great deal of anecdotal evidence suggests the effect is indeed comparable. There is just no doubt that the children who attend their parents' college-in-prison graduations, and excitedly try on their caps and gowns or carry their diplomas, are being sent a positive message about the value of staying in school and getting a good education.

Dorell Smallwood is one formerly incarcerated parent who exemplifies many of these positive effects. While he was in prison, he served time in the same facility where his father was being held. Unlike his father, however, Dorell went to college and was able to land a job supervising the prison's laundry, which enabled him to save enough to send his daughter $2,000 to help with her college tuition. In addition to underscoring the benefits to families, his story demonstrates how those returning home from prison with the skills and new perspectives gained in college can lend strength to their communities, often helping young people to negotiate their way successfully through the risks they face in the impoverished communities from which so many of the incarcerated come.

Dorell grew up in a tough, poverty-stricken neighborhood of Brooklyn, New York. His father was seventeen and his mother was fifteen when he was born in 1976. While he was still an infant, his father went to prison, where he has spent most of his time ever since and where he remains today. His mother was a bastion of support and a positive role model. She held various jobs—in neighborhood stores, as a phone operator with AT&T, and as a receptionist at a law firm. Then, in 1994, she began a twenty-year career as a New York City police officer.

Even with his mother's example, and even though he loved school and participated in lots of after-school activities, by the time he was fifteen, Dorell was on his way to joining his father in prison. "Crime was all around me in the Fort Greene projects," he recalls. He wanted "cash to buy materialistic things" and looked up to the neighborhood drug dealers. Soon, he was spending most of his time hanging out with friends, smoking pot, and selling drugs. In 1991, he was arrested for possession of a gun and released to the custody of his mother. In 1993, he was shot five times while going to a movie with friends as part of what he describes as "an earlier neighborhood beef between guys from rival Brooklyn neighborhoods" that had resulted in a homicide. He was arrested while recovering from those gunshot wounds, convicted, and sentenced to twenty years.

In prison, Dorell decided that after he was released he wanted to work with young people so that they might avoid the mistakes he had made. With that in mind, he applied to the Bard Prison Initiative—"a place where I was fully a student, not an inmate," he says—and was admitted. Now, with a bachelor's degree from Bard as well as a master's in professional studies from the New York Theological Seminary, he is working as an advocate for young people at Brooklyn Defender Services, helping others who have become involved with the criminal justice system. Going to college in prison enabled him to find his way out of the repeating cycles of crime and imprisonment that have dominated his father's life and the lives of many others in neighborhoods like the one in which he came of age.[35]

Men and women who return from prison ready to build productive new lives can make important contributions to their communities. Vastly disproportionate numbers of them come from neighborhoods of concentrated poverty, which have been ravaged by the illicit drug trade, a massive flight of jobs out of cities, gang violence and other criminal activity, and failing schools. W.E.B. Du Bois writes in his classic *The Souls of Black Folk*, "The chief problem in any community cursed with crime is not the punishment of the criminals, but the preventing of the young from being trained to crime."[36] Positive role models of educational achievement, who can demonstrate that getting a good education can help people beat the odds stacked against them, are vital to at-risk youth. By setting such an example and actively mentoring young people, the graduates of college-in-prison programs can help to play the role in these communities that, as urban anthropologist Elijah Anderson describes, was once played by the "old heads." Anderson explains, "The old head was once the epitome of decency in inner-city neighborhoods. . . . His acknowledged role in the community was to teach, support, encourage, and, in effect, socialize young men to meet their responsibilities regarding work, family life, the law, and common decency."[37] According to Anderson, as a large portion of the middle-class residents of these neighborhoods moved out over the past decades, and as job flight and the drug economy devastated these communities, the role of the old heads was diminished.

Those who return from prison with a deep dedication to the benefits of learning and a commitment to avoid any further involvement in crime can speak with particular authority about the difficulties of going to prison and the need to study hard and to steer clear of trouble with the law. In these neighborhoods, too often, those who return from prison go right back to criminal activity—put another way, crime spills out of the prisons and back into the streets. It is a vicious circle. Many young people, especially boys of color, are socialized from an early age to go to prison. For them, imprisonment has become a rite of passage. The attraction of the street has undermined the prestige and authority of exemplars of maturity and stability, and many of the youth in these neighborhoods are hostile to authority and rebel against it in ways that harm others and themselves. Many see the schools as "outposts" of mainstream society and resist their requirements and demands.[38] People like Dorell Smallwood can offer positive models that exemplify the benefits of staying in school.

In addition, formerly incarcerated men and women can bring

special insight to addressing problems of high-crime neighborhoods. The late Eddie Ellis, who died in 2014, is an example. He grew up in Harlem, helped to found the Black Panther Party there, and was then convicted of murder and sentenced to twenty-five years in prison, after which he founded and led a number of organizations to cut incarceration rates and improve conditions of confinement, including the Community Justice Center, the Prison Moratorium Project, and the Center for NuLeadership on Urban Solutions. While he was in prison, he had managed to secure a transfer to Sing Sing in order to attend the master's program offered by the New York Theological Seminary and then joined with fellow "prisoner-scholars" in a think tank at the Green Haven Correctional Facility to examine the home addresses of people incarcerated in New York. Their analysis, which revealed that some 75 percent of the people in custody came from just seven neighborhoods in New York City, launched Ellis into a lifelong quest for criminal justice reform.[39]

Other graduates of college-in-prison programs have likewise dedicated themselves to finding ways to understand and address the problems that lead so many in these impoverished communities into trouble, both before and after spending time away. Mark Graham, who spent twenty years in prison, knew how critical the need for safe, free, immediate housing is for those released from prison and founded the Redemption Center in the Ocean Hill–Brownsville neighborhood of Brooklyn, after he was released. It provides short-term housing for prison returnees. Graham grew up in East New York and Bedford-Stuyvesant, two of Brooklyn's toughest neighborhoods, and began to get into trouble for stealing, shoplifting, drinking, and smoking pot when he was twelve. His mother turned to the courts for help, and he was placed in various group homes. They were "finishing schools for felons," he recalls, with guys from all the boroughs of New York swapping stories about different crimes. Then, when he was just sixteen, things got worse. With several friends, he tried to rob a man and ended up shooting him by mistake, and it was this that resulted in a twenty-year sentence for Mark.[40]

While he was incarcerated, he earned a GED, followed by advanced degrees, including a bachelor's and a master's in professional studies. When he was released in the fall of 2001, he turned to Julio Medina, whom he had gotten to know when he was in the next cell at Sing Sing as well as a classmate in the master's program there. Medina had founded Exodus Transitional Community three years earlier to provide services for people returning from prison. He hired Mark to be a case manager. Four years later, Mark went out on his own, opening the Redemption Center. The men and women live on different floors, with shared rooms equipped with a bed and mattress for each person and not much more. The services are minimal, and strict rules are enforced: everyone must be involved in jobs or training from 9 a.m. to 3 p.m. and be in the house by 9 p.m. The residents do not complain; they credit Mark with helping them "get back in step" and almost none have gone back to prison. Reflecting on the work Mark and he are doing, Medina says, "We use our passion to help. Through our own wounds, we are able to go out and heal others."[41] That is certainly true, but it is also the case that both men received an advanced education while incarcerated.

Still another way in which those who participate in college while in prison are contributing to the welfare of their communities is by taking jobs in various social service organizations. Cheryl Wilkins is one example. She was part of the group of women at the Bedford Hills facility who wrote the mission statement that led to the reestablishment of a college program there after the 1994 Pell cutoff. The women focused on the importance of going to college as a means to empower them "to truly pay our debt to society by repairing some of what has been broken."[42] Wilkins is doing that as a senior program manager at the Center for Justice at Columbia University, where, among other things, she provides training for high school guidance counselors and school principals about how to work with youth with family members in prison. She wants to end the school-to-prison pipeline. Her responsibilities also include helping the incarcerated return home successfully and coordinating the Healing Communities Network Program, which facilitates support groups both inside prisons and back in the communities.

Many of those who participate in college while in prison take jobs in established social service organizations. Sean Pica, the director of the Hudson Link college program, reports that the majority of their graduates have gone to work for such agencies. Many college-in-prison graduates have found such work because people managing socially concerned and advocacy organizations rarely subscribe to the stereotypes that keep a large number of other employers from hiring people with criminal records. Equally important, the jobs are offered to them because experienced professionals in these fields understand that the formerly incarcerated can bring especially rich insights and special sensitivity to the work as well as a great deal of passion. If and when financial aid to those in prison is renewed, more people released from prison will likely take up work that addresses the many causes and consequences of poverty and crime.

Mitigating the damaging spillover effects of mass incarceration for individuals, their families, and whole communities is one of the greatest challenges facing this country. College-in-prison programs can contribute significantly to meeting that challenge, and can do so in many different ways. They are a social investment that promises large returns.

5

Democracy and Education

The Civic Imperative for College in Prison

Erica Mateo is building an outstanding career as a civic leader in Brownsville, New York, the troubled neighborhood where she grew up. She is regularly quoted in the press on issues of concern to her neighbors; she has designed programs to help young people develop a sense of responsibility for their actions; and she has led campaigns aimed at combating the gun and gang violence that has made Brownsville one of New York's most dangerous places.

Mateo has always cared about her neighborhood, but she is convinced that the college education she began while serving time at the Bayview Correctional Facility in New York City gave her the skills, confidence, and knowledge needed to take on the challenges associated with community-building work. Her experience with the Bard Prison Initiative at Bayview ignited an intense interest in anthropology, and after release, she finished her bachelor's degree at Bard's main campus in Annandale-on-Hudson, and then returned to Brownsville to do community renewal work.

She landed a job at the Brownsville Community Justice Center, one of the programs run by the Center for Court Innovation, a nonprofit that works closely with the New York State court system to develop new approaches to problems in criminal justice, from juvenile delinquency to community reentry for the incarcerated. Starting as a program associate, assisting the managing director, she was quickly promoted to the job of case manager, directly counseling young people who had run into trouble with the law. Within a year, she had been promoted again, to the role of coordinator of an antiviolence project. This project brought together local residents and representatives of city agencies to plan the steps necessary to revitalize Brownsville, where many buildings had been ravaged by the waves of arson that flared up in New York City in the 1970s and where, in subsequent decades, drug addiction and crime had become endemic. She was so successful in leading that yearlong initiative that she was again promoted, this time to managing all community programs for the center.[1]

One of the programs she has helped launch is a youth court. Through the court, young people in the community aged ten to eighteen who are accused of committing infractions, such as vandalism, disorderly conduct, or truancy, are sent by the school system, the police department, or the family court system to be tried by a jury of their peers. The teen jurors, also from the community, are trained by the center to be community advocates who can discuss the harm that destructive behavior can cause. According to Erica, the program's goal is to make the court system "more community-centric . . . so the community can be more involved in what's happening in the court system, and in the response to crime and safety in their neighborhood."[2] One of her hopes is that through this program, people in the community will learn that they have a major stake in the "crime and safety" of their neighborhood.

Erica has also been involved in projects the center is spearheading aimed at economic development. She reports that one of these, a mentoring program that teams up young people in the community with successful entrepreneurs, who help them to pursue ideas for businesses and coach them about the requirements of running one, has been enormously popular. Another, the Belmont Revitalization

Project, is designed to stimulate the restoration of Belmont Avenue, once a vibrant shopping street running through the heart of the neighborhood, which has become a depressing and dangerous stretch of blocks with many boarded-up buildings. This project is close to her heart, since she grew up right around the corner from Belmont Avenue and fondly remembers it as a thriving neighborhood hub.[3] The work Erica is doing both helps to improve the lives of many individuals and plays a vital role in rebuilding trust and common cause among all the residents of Brownsville, rekindling their sense of community. The projects she is involved with are also increasing understanding and trust between the residents of Brownsville and the larger society.

In addition to improving the employment prospects of people who have been to prison, changing prison environments, and having a salutary effect on prisoners' families, college-in-prison programs can offer students the knowledge and skills they will need to serve their communities as active, engaged citizens. College-in-prison programs promote civic competence and support student aspirations to make a positive difference for other people. Many incarcerated students are eager to become leaders in the improvement of their neighborhoods. Some want to help young people stay on the right side of the law. Others want to find ways to ease the difficulties faced by families with a mother or father in prison. Still others are fired up about becoming public advocates for causes, such as school improvement or changes in drug laws. In college, incarcerated men and women can acquire the communication skills and broadened perspectives that will enable them to pursue such civic ambitions effectively. For others, college provides the inspiration to become more politically engaged, helping them better understand how civic institutions operate and how they can participate in making them more effective.

The responsibility of colleges to promote civic engagement has become a matter of considerable interest in the higher-education community. Until recently, civic education was a required course of study almost exclusively in elementary and secondary schools, and generally taught at the college level in courses taken by students in majors such as political science, sociology, and philosophy, or as electives. But today, more colleges are actively encouraging public service among their students and have created service-learning programs, which send students out into communities to do volunteer work. Some even make community service a requirement. For example, Tulane University in New Orleans mandates that all undergraduates must complete one service-learning course, while Augsburg College in Minneapolis incorporates public-service projects into many of its classes and encourages its students to work in the community.

Among the higher-education leaders championing this cause, none has been more central than Thomas Ehrlich, a former president of Indiana University, who served as a senior scholar at the Carnegie Foundation for the Advancement of Teaching. Ehrlich's widely cited definition of civic engagement speaks aptly to why participation in public affairs is such a vital component of a well-functioning democracy. He defines a "civically responsible individual" as one who recognizes his or her connection to "a larger social fabric and therefore considers social problems to be at least partly his or her own."[4] Civically responsible people, he maintains, understand the social and moral dimensions of common problems and feel a responsibility "to take action" to address them.[5]

For students going to college in prison, civic education is especially critical since few of them had previous opportunities in school to learn about the operation of the U.S. government or to study social problems, including those related to social class and race, which have often been central in their own lives. This does not mean that civic education should necessarily be organized as a distinct part of the curriculum. Classes in history, philosophy, literature, psychology, economics, sociology, anthropology, and

many other subject areas often deepen student interest in public problems by offering new theories or perspectives. Classes in
business, architecture, and public health, to name just a few, can
also have this effect. Insight into social problems sometimes comes
in the most unexpected ways. In an introduction to anthropology
class that Erica Mateo took while still in custody at Bayview, for
instance, she became fascinated by an ethnography she read of
an Eskimo woman. She realized, she explains looking back, that
"life did not have to be as it was." The conditions of life, she now
saw, are not set in stone. That understanding further sparked her
awakening recognition that she could play a part in changing all
that made life so difficult for people in depressed urban neighborhoods. Later, while studying at Bard's main campus, she also took a
writing class that she believes helped her find ways to use her own
"voice" to advocate for causes about which she feels passionately.[6]

Another Bard student, who took a class I taught entitled "John
Dewey and His Contemporaries," had a similar experience as a
result of discussing Dewey's conception of ethics. "I've been locked
up since I was seventeen," he told me one day. "Before that, I moved
around a lot, through foster families and group homes. So I knew
how the world *did* work, but before reading Dewey, I had not realized that things aren't as they are *meant* ideally to be. Now I have a
road map for what I want to do to make the ideal more real."[7] Since
going home, he has spent most of his time finishing his college degree, but he has also been giving lectures to church groups about
the importance of taking responsibility for the well-being of one's
community.

Other formerly incarcerated students have also described the
ways in which college classes increased their sense of civic responsibility. Michael Friday, another college alum who earned a
degree while incarcerated, talks about college having made him
see the importance of not only participation in politics, but even
beyond that "intelligent participation" grounded in "facts and not

media-driven fictions." He now believes, he says, that "if you understand the world, you will understand the role you can and must play in it."[8] David Basile, a student of the Prison University Project at San Quentin, asserts that his experience in college "has caused a paradigm shift in the way I view the inequalities suffered by minorities in our culture." Explaining the change, he said, "Listening, healthy debates and openmindedness—principles instilled by the faculty—have encouraged my departure from decades-long anti-social beliefs and actions."[9] Students sometimes also discuss the importance of college classes in teaching them about the way society operates and how they must adhere to its laws and respect public mores in order to be successful when they go home. One college-in-prison student, a former drug dealer, explained in an interview on National Public Radio that, after studying history, economics, psychology, environmentalism, African and Asian politics, and the thirteenth-century Mongols, he was now "in a position . . . to be able to see the world in the way that I should have seen it years ago. It's a little bit easier for me to navigate through society."[10]

Dorell Smallwood, who works with the Brooklyn Defender Services, recalls a civics class that had a great impact on him. It apparently helped him realize that liberal democracy by its nature has excluded some groups while enfranchising others. At the same time, he stresses that as much as such specific insights into the political system were important to him, it was the overall experience, "the totality of his classes," that, in his words, "made the world more accessible to analyze." That capacity, he observes, gave him the confidence to believe "that wherever (professionally) I landed in the world/society, I was equipped to learn and understand the functionality of it."[11] This sense of mastery, this confidence in one's ability to discern how things work, this understanding of the rules of the game, is the bedrock of a feeling of civic belonging, which is, in turn, a prerequisite for active civic participation.

In their study of the college program at Bedford Hills, Michelle

Fine and her colleagues also noted a relationship between gaining confidence in one's understanding and intelligence and acquiring a sense of legitimacy to comment on public issues. Fine and the team she led reported that the college program helped the women to see themselves in line with earlier women who had struggled and accomplished great things. The 1999 valedictorian expressed this eloquently in her commencement speech, referring to the long list of women who struggled to win political enfranchisement as well as her fellow graduates as "women who are standing firm and who believe in our ability to achieve, even in the face of political, legislative, economic, and social obstacles. We too are women who have decided that we believe in ourselves and in our worth as human beings. . . . So, like the other great women who went before us . . . we have actively determined to change the course of our lives, and in so doing, we have begun to change the course of history for all women. . . . [We] have found our voices and our place as women, [women] who will *not* move to the back of *any* bus."[12]

The power of college-in-prison programs to magnify their students' sense of responsibility to contribute to society was described particularly well by a student in the Notre Dame–Holy Cross College program at the Westville Correctional Facility in Indiana in his commencement speech. He pointed out that there was an "underlying theme" running through all the classes. There was frequent discussion of inequality and social responsibility and ways individuals can make a difference for other people in their community. Speaking with unusual candor, he then explained that he and his classmates were especially touched by these discussions because they knew their past actions had caused pain and suffering for people they loved and were eager to find ways to make restitution. College, he noted, equipped them to return to society and make their families proud.[13]

Most incarcerated students, like their peers on the outside, enroll in college primarily in the hope of boosting their employment prospects. But many come to see the enhanced civic understanding and increased sense of belonging they gain in college as crucial to the future course they set for themselves after release. As previously noted, the fact that many of them find work in the social services, often in counseling, legal aid, or health services, is partly due to fewer barriers to entrance into jobs in those areas. But it is also due to the commitment of these men and women to help others and improve society. This is often born in the regret many feel about the harm they have caused other people, and then is heightened as their college experience enables them to identify causes in which they can invest themselves and roles they can assume. College-in-prison graduates have expressed their sense of civic responsibility in varied ways, with some even going into research, analysis, and advocacy concerning public problems and their possible solutions.

With their firsthand knowledge of the conditions of confinement and, in too many cases, their personal experiences with the failings of our civic institutions, men and women who have spent time in prison can offer especially insightful ideas about how to make improvements. Glenn E. Martin is doing that today. He has devoted his career since release from prison to studying, and speaking out about, the importance of helping the incarcerated and formerly incarcerated play significant roles in criminal justice reform. He spent six years in prison on an armed robbery conviction. Today, he leads a nonprofit organization he founded in 2014, called JustLeadershipUSA, which aims to cut the number of people in prison by 50 percent by 2030, through advocacy work and training.

"Since the day in 1995 when the handcuffs first bound my wrists," Glenn has written, working to mitigate what he describes as the "hypocrisy and insidiousness of our criminal justice system" has been his mission in life.[14] He believes passionately that justice requires that men and women who have known the criminal justice system from the inside be given prime responsibility for shaping criminal justice laws and institutions, including prisons. He

has won numerous awards from organizations involved in criminal justice reform and been asked to advise many public officials,
including President Obama, about matters related to crime and
criminal punishment. He gives much of the credit for his success
as a consultant and organizational leader to the liberal arts education he received through Canisius College, a Jesuit institution that
runs a college program at the Wyoming Correctional Facility near
Buffalo, where he was being held. He speaks eloquently about the
debates he had with his college classmates, and how those discussions offered degrees of intellectual freedom he had never known
before. Growing up in the Bedford-Stuyvesant neighborhood of
Brooklyn, New York, he had felt called upon to voice only those
opinions that were sanctioned by his peers, either respectfully expressed to elders or more colloquially to one another. It was clear
that his friends expected him to accept and repeat their belief in
black oppression. In college, he was able to think for himself and to
speak candidly even when his views differed from those of his professors or classmates. Glenn maintains that college classes helped
him see beyond the "us versus them" mentality that he had previously been expected to maintain. Studying history, and in particular learning about the Holocaust, he says, opened his eyes to the
oppression and prejudice others beside young African Americans
had suffered at the hands of the more powerful.

Glenn Martin's postcollege experience speaks both to the barriers that even those who are college educated run up against during
reentry and to how well suited their education makes them for
civic work. Glenn was turned down by at least forty potential employers before he finally landed a job with the Legal Action Center, a nonprofit based in New York City that fights discrimination
against people who have been incarcerated, as well as those with
HIV/AIDs or drug addiction. While working there, he founded
the H.I.R.E. Network (Helping Individuals with Criminal Records Reenter Through Employment). From there, he moved to

a job at the Fortune Society, which helps people coming home from prison and is staffed largely by formerly incarcerated men and women, and remained there for seven years, deeply involved in advocacy for the rights of the formerly incarcerated. Building on those experiences, in 2014 he founded JustLeaderhipUSA, an organization designed to enable "those closest to the problem," namely the formerly incarcerated, to acquire the knowledge and skills necessary to gain credibility in working toward a solution for overincarceration.

Martin has said that while in prison he discovered that most of his peers realized they had broken the social contract and wanted to find ways to give back. Today, JustLeadershipUSA provides leadership training in public speaking, grant writing, and management to help them take on publicly significant projects and to gain standing as experts on issues about which they know a great deal. As of March 2016, the organization had enrolled 124 men and women in its programs in three cities (New York, St. Louis, and Washington, D.C.) In addition, Martin and others had presented the case for involving more formerly incarcerated people in policy work through media outlets ranging from the *Wall Street Journal* to *Ebony Magazine* to *The Daily Show with Jon Stewart*. Martin has written, spoken, and blogged about the importance of restoring Pell Grants to prisoners, cutting mandatory minimum sentences, and restoring full voting rights to all people who have been in prison. The organization he now leads and the positions he is fighting for will strengthen the representativeness of American democracy by ensuring that the voices of those in groups most likely to be affected by criminal justice policies play a significant role in designing those policies.[15]

For Erica Mateo, Dorell Smallwood, Glenn E. Martin, and many other college-in-prison graduates, civic engagement has become a career. But it need not be a full-time, professional pursuit. Some formerly imprisoned college students have chosen to give back through volunteering in schools, hospitals, libraries, or other non-profit organizations. Raymond Roe, who participated in the Cornell college program at Auburn prison in New York, works in a full-time, paid position for the Red Cross helping run blood drives during the day. Then, in the evening and on weekends, he spends as much time as possible talking with at-risk kids. He once told a reporter that it is now his "mission to share his experience with young people." Having spent "most of my life behind a wall," he explained, "the little bit I have left, I want to make the best of it." A big part of that is talking with young people about the mistakes he made, in the hope that hearing about his experience will keep them on the right side of the law.[16]

Like more traditional colleges, college-in-prison programs approach civic education in different ways. Some put explicit emphasis on teaching civics and encouraging students to become involved in social change, while others do not, although they offer many classes that may inspire civic interests. The Freedom Education Project at the University of Puget Sound, founded by Tanya Erzen, a scholar of religion and gender at the university, is one of those that teaches civics directly. As described by Erzen, one goal of the program is to help students see "their experiences as fundamentally social and political," so that they can come to understand better the larger forces that shape individual actions. Another main goal is to equip them with "a voice" to speak about "what goes on" in this country, as one of her students puts it.[17]

The Freedom Education Project teaches civics not only in this direct way but also through the underlying emphasis running throughout the curriculum on building a sense of empowerment and self-efficacy in the all-female student body. One of the core classes is "Gender, Politics, and Citizenship in U.S. History," which covers a wide range of topics, moving from different conceptions of citizenship to the history of welfare in the United States. The students are challenged to articulate their own conceptions of

democratic rights and responsibilities. They also study Huey Newton and Bobby Seale's ten-point platform for the Black Panther
Party, and then compose their own ten-point manifesto focused on
conditions in the Washington Corrections Center, where they are
imprisoned—a powerful way to convey how the tools of civic engagement can be directed to the circumstances of one's own daily
life. Another class teaches what the program refers to as "civil survival," which prepares students for the many practical challenges of
reentering life on the outside, including how to secure child support and housing assistance.

The program at Grinnell College, which is the only college-in-
prison program in the state of Iowa and offers classes in a number of prisons, takes another approach. It is designed to facilitate
what is referred to as "reciprocal learning" between students on
Grinnell's main campus, who participate as instructors, tutors, and
program coordinators, and students in the prison. The hope is to
inspire an interest in public affairs and active citizenship in both
groups. There is no special emphasis on civic education in the curriculum, which offers a traditional liberal arts mix of classes, from
neuroscience to economics and the classics. Reports by those who
have participated indicate that the program is achieving its goal.

For the incarcerated students, getting to know Grinnell students
who have never been convicted of a crime brings a glimpse of a
way of living and of opportunities that they had either never understood before or never thought they could attain. Michael Cosby,
who went through Grinnell's First Year of College program at the
Newton Correctional Facility in Jasper County, Iowa, has stated
that the program gave him "an appreciation for the way the other
half lives—[even] that there is another half." That has inspired him
to help other incarcerated students with their papers and will likely
continue to lead him into service activities once he is home.[18]

For their part, many of the roughly fifty nonincarcerated Grinnell students who have volunteered each semester to teach, tutor,

or otherwise help run the program have indicated that they have developed a powerful calling to do socially engaged work—more than half of them have reported to the college that, as a result of their experience in the prisons, they have become teachers or social workers, or have become involved in work with the prison system or with issues faced by the incarcerated. One alumnus who is leading a project that documents the histories of prisons in New York State stated that the prison program had shaped his career interests and choices more than just about anything else he did at Grinnell.

The Bard Prison Initiative has no explicit civic education requirement, but many of the classes cover aspects of civics in discussions of social issues, and some have put the focus squarely on civics. A lawyer by training, Daniel Karpowitz has written about his experience at Bard in his book *Reading In: College in Prison in an Age of Mass Incarceration* (forthcoming, 2017). He describes a class he used to teach called "Civics and the American Political Tradition," which included readings from Thomas Hobbes's *Leviathan* and Milton Friedman's *Capitalism and Freedom*, among others, and queried the nature of citizenship, democracy, and liberalism. More than providing basic information about the structure of American government, the course was designed to suggest to students that in thinking about government, one must consider human nature.[19]

In the classes I have taught, not only the ones about progressive social thought, but also those about education and social policy, we have talked frequently about the meaning of community, civil rights, participation, democracy, equality, and freedom. We may go over fundamental matters, such as how a law moves through Congress or how a court case reaches the Supreme Court, but such nuts-and-bolts topics are a prelude to more open-ended discussions of contentious questions. Can a democracy exist if inequality is as extreme as it is in the United States today? Do citizens owe each other a common standard of living? Should the federal government become involved in public school curricula? Does everyone have a right to go to college? Whatever the question and whatever the answer, students learn to expect a "But why?" response. I am not teaching civics directly, but I am hoping to teach an appreciation for complexity and differences of opinion in serious debate about public affairs.

The Bard Prison Initiative also offers a number of extracurricular activities that promote civic engagement. One of these is the Bard Debate Union, which David Register, its director, describes as intended "to provide a robust civic education, in which students learn how to engage in their own governance."[20] Each semester, in weekly meetings, roughly fifteen students discuss the topic assigned for their next debate. They also argue over the relevance of various articles they have read and generate strategies for presenting their arguments. They then each give a presentation of the best argument they have come up with for their position, and they critique one another, with usually four of them selected for the actual debate.

The debaters typically spend hundreds of hours over three or four months preparing. According to Register, their preparation does not end when formal sessions are complete. "They talk debate in their cells, the yard and the mess hall," he says. "They verbally spar with BPI students who are not on the debate team, and talk with their families—creating for themselves a group of informal coaches." The topics they have debated have ranged from "Should NATO be immediately disbanded?" to "Should public schools in the United States have the ability to deny enrollment to undocumented students?" With victories over such outstanding debate teams as West Point and Harvard, and a record of many more wins than losses, the Bard debaters have clearly learned to make the kinds of well-researched and persuasive arguments that are central to working for social change.[21]

Whether or not colleges in prisons specifically tutor students in the knowledge and skills that define civic competence, perhaps by teaching about the history of social movements or about the tactics of protest, these programs prepare their students to take effective social action. This may involve organizing a public campaign to reinstate the vote for people with felony convictions in states where they are disenfranchised, lobbying the city, state, or federal government to support prison reform, or engaging on a smaller local scale, as Erica Mateo did by organizing a cleanup day in which 150 residents of Brownsville helped pick up trash and clean buildings along her beloved Belmont Avenue. Whatever the form, such active involvement in public issues demonstrates what civic education can contribute to incarcerated college students and, through them, to all of us. The more those who are incarcerated are given opportunities to learn how to articulate grievances persuasively and to acquire the skills of civic literacy and action, the more men and women like Glenn E. Martin and Erica Mateo there will be, people who are committed to helping make much-needed change happen.

Formerly incarcerated college graduates are especially well equipped to help mediate conflicts between the police and local citizens and to advise public officials about situations that undermine a community's trust in government. Understanding the causes of the many problems and social injustices that are troubling so many people in the United States and around the world requires well-informed, critical analysis and empathetic, respectful discussion. Fathoming the structural causes that have led to job flight and to the decaying of whole inner-city neighborhoods demands careful reading, thinking, listening, and research. The same might be said of the problems facing public schools and hospitals. People who have been to college in prison are prime candidates for helping their neighbors speak out about these matters. They also have a particularly powerful perspective from which to explain the tragic consequences of mass incarceration and the need for policy reform. Unless people know how to gain a hearing for their concerns peacefully, and how to take constructive, nonviolent action to push for the changes they think are needed, some of them will inevitably turn to violent means of protest. Many more will simply opt out of engagement with the issues and any efforts to address them.

Instilling a sense of civic belonging and inspiring more engagement in all citizens should be a central mission for this country—it is necessary to the survival of a democratic way of life—but encouraging civic connections is particularly important for the formerly incarcerated because they are marginalized in so many ways. Those who have served time and are no longer in prison are still "locked out" of full citizenship, to borrow the title of a book by sociologists Jeff Manza and Christopher Uggen. Incarceration is, of course, a purposeful mechanism of separation from society. Unfortunately, however, in the United States today, that separation continues even after those who have been released return home. As Manza and Uggen have shown, many of the country's laws deny basic rights of citizenship to those who have been convicted of a felony, in some instances for the rest of their lives. This makes them what can only be described as "partial citizens."[22]

Formerly incarcerated men and women—even those who have been equipped through a college education to be active, intelligent citizens—are banned from voting in many states and prohibited from participation in several of our most basic democratic processes, including serving on juries and holding public office. According to the Brennan Center for Justice, some 6 million Americans cannot vote as a result of a current or past felony conviction, and 4.4 million of these people have finished serving their sentences. Laws bar former felons from many types of work. One list included up to eight hundred occupations.[23] Provisions vary across the states, but in many of them people who have been convicted of felonies cannot work in the securities field, in banking, or in public schools. In some states they cannot work as home health aides. In

New York, they cannot own a barbershop or become an emergency medical technician; in Florida, they cannot be an acupuncturist, a speech pathologist, or a cosmetologist; and in Illinois, they are banned from jobs as varied as pet shop owner, roofer, dietician, and architect.[24] In *American Citizenship: The Quest for Inclusion*, political theorist Judith Shklar observes that opportunities to earn and to vote are "the two great emblems of public standing."[25] Depriving the formerly incarcerated of the most basic rights and responsibilities of citizenship undermines possibilities for what Manza and Uggen call "civic reintegration."[26] They believe that general education combined with civic education, with political participation added into the mix, would actually promote desistance from crime.

For men and women coming home from prison, there should be opportunities to build new lives that include joining in the neighborhood projects and electoral decisions that shape public policy. That is especially the case for people who have been to college in prison, since that is likely to have fostered an active commitment to advancing social justice and the common good. Erica Mateo says that she has only begun her work. "I've grown and I'm grateful," she explains, "and I am also energized and looking to take on new challenges." She may not remain in Brownsville. She is eager to see if she "can take what I've learned . . . to another NYC community or another urban community outside NYC."[27] Acting in support of more equality and greater opportunity for all will likely be her lifelong quest. Providing people in prison with access to college is a wise investment in fostering a democratic way of life.

6

The Challenge of College in Prison

Insights from History

Since the mid-1970s, the proposition that people in prison should be offered access to education has met with widespread skepticism. Criticism of education programs in prisons has a long history, but it gained traction in the 1970s due in large part to an influential article by a little-known criminologist named Robert Martinson. Published in 1974 in *The Public Interest*, the article presented an abbreviated version of the results of a meta-analysis that reanalyzed the findings of a large group of studies. In this case, the focus of the reanalysis was the effects of a wide range of types of prison programs on rates of recidivism.

Martinson led a team of researchers in a review of 231 evaluations of prison programs, referred to in the report as "treatments," which had been published between 1945 and 1967. The programs studied included everything from so-called academic education to vocational training, psychological counseling, and hormone therapy. The impact on recidivism was the only outcome considered. How those who had gone through different types of programs had adjusted to prison life, or had achieved postprison vocational success, or had adapted to life back in their home communities after release were all ignored. That was true even though those were outcomes toward which many of the programs had been explicitly directed. The bottom line of the report, which ran to fourteen hundred pages, was that "with few and isolated exceptions," none of the interventions "had an appreciable effect on recidivism."[1]

The report was not published until 1975, and Martinson had decided before then to write his *Public Interest* piece, as well as a number of other articles for both academic and popular journals, in order to get word about the findings out to a wide audience. He began writing the articles because he objected to many of the programs, which he and other critics argued were coercive and violated the rights of prisoners.

Long before writing the *Public Interest* essay, while a student at the University of California, Martinson had traveled to Mississippi with a group of Freedom Riders. He was arrested in Jackson and sent to Parchman State Prison Farm, which turned his interests toward criminology.[2] The harshness of the treatment of prisoners there led him to the conclusion that efforts to rehabilitate prisoners were no less coercive than earlier forms of corporal punishment. When he joined the evaluation group in New York six years later, in 1967, he brought that critical perspective with him.

Though Martinson cautioned in the *Public Interest* article that many of the studies examined were flawed, and that "it is just possible that some of our treatment programs *are* working to some extent," newspaper headlines boiled down his argument to the simple, unequivocal phrase "nothing works." Politicians took this as a slogan and it became a widely quoted summation of the findings of the report.

The conclusions of both the Martinson article and the official report, which has become known as the Martinson Report, were subsequently found to be fundamentally flawed; many of the studies examined had been poorly conducted and violated standards of scientific research. In addition, the official report stated that the findings did not indicate that nothing *could* work to reduce recidivism. It merely said that "the field of corrections has not as yet found satisfying ways to reduce recidivism by satisfying amounts."[3] That was a long way from "nothing works," but, by the time the report was published, popular understanding had settled on that phrase. That unfortunate distortion must be corrected, if current consideration of restoring access to college for the incarcerated is to be based on accurate information.

Solid research has now shown that higher education in prison has significant, positive effects not only on recidivism but also on prospects for postrelease employment, ease of reentry, and participation in all sorts of public causes. The skepticism about education programs, and the strenuous objections to them that Martinson and others voiced in the 1970s, stemmed, in part, from the fact that many efforts to translate rehabilitative ideals into practice were flawed in execution. In particular, Martinson came to realize that many of the rehabilitative programs to which he objected shared one fundamental weakness: they were coercive.

By their very nature, of course, prisons are places of coercion. They are institutions to which one is sentenced for purposes of punishment. In consequence, efforts at rehabilitation have often been conceived of and viewed as part of a punishment regime, and for that reason have been met with hostility by the incarcerated, sometimes leading to the breaking of rules, violence, and even riots. That response has, in turn, led to frustration on the part of the men and women who have designed and run rehabilitative activities, often believing that they were acting out of kindness and benevolence. Only on the relatively rare occasions when reformers have managed to make participation in such activities a matter of choice and personal agency has education had discernibly positive outcomes. The story of past efforts to offer education to the incarcerated thus offers a cautionary tale. It demonstrates that to promote the kind of economic, social, and civic benefits of which it is capable, education in prison requires autonomy, freedom, and opportunities to exercise self-direction even while students are still confined.

To begin the story of education in American prisons, it is helpful to understand that we began as a "convict nation," a point University of Pennsylvania political scientist Marie Gottschalk emphasizes in her history of the politics of mass incarceration. We may celebrate the Puritans, who came freely to New England to build "a city on a hill," but the fact is that by the 1650s most of the British settlers to North America were transported felons or their children. They brought a strict code of morals with them, as well as harsh English criminal punishment practices.[4] Fines were common for minor offenses, and more significant infractions often led to corporal punishment, public shaming, and enforced labor, with the worst offenses leading to confinement, banishment, or death. Physical punishments were brutal, with offenders being flogged, branded, maimed, dunked, or placed in the stocks. Some were hanged, often with raucous crowds gathering to witness the event. Jails and prisons were more common in the colonies than hospitals or schools.[5]

Soon after the revolution, things began to change. Many of the Founding Fathers agreed with Thomas Jefferson's belief that "cruel and sanguinary laws defeat their own purpose."[6] Echoing his compatriot Jefferson, the Philadelphia physician Benjamin Rush, who served in the Second Continental Congress and was a signer of the Declaration of Independence, maintained that capital punishment was barbaric and a throwback to monarchical government. A Quaker, Rush advocated a more benevolent approach to punishment. For those criminals who might be reformed, he recommended imprisonment in a "house of repentance."[7] In a letter to one of his British correspondents, he claimed that, "a prison sometimes supplies the place of a church and out preaches the preacher in conveying useful instruction to the heart."[8] In 1787, together with other prison reform advocates in the city, many of them also

Quakers, Rush helped establish the Society for Alleviating the Miseries of Public Prisons.

Three years later the society secured passage of a change in the penal code of Pennsylvania, which transformed the Walnut Street jail in Philadelphia into a state-run prison, with a new wing called the "Penitentiary House." Here, according to the statute, "more hardened and atrocious offenders" were held individually, in small cells, rather than together in large rooms, as in the rest of the prison. Strict rules of behavior were instituted for the entire prison population, which called for prisoners to refrain from speaking profanities and from indecent behavior, with punishment for infractions often being time in the solitary cells.[9] The idea was that prisons should induce penitence in prisoners for their sins by imposing time to reflect in quiet on their crimes. Hard labor carried out in silence was also believed to induce reformation, with all prisoners required to work long hours at trades, such as making nails, sawing stones, weaving, and carding wool. In addition, supplementary instruction in morals and religion through Bible reading was mandated.

The Walnut Street model was quickly copied in other states, the idea taking hold that prisoners should do penance for crimes, and prisons coming commonly to be called penitentiaries. Though intended to offer more humane treatment than earlier jails, the penitentiaries were plagued with problems from the start. Overcrowding undermined plans for silent work and reflection, as solitary cells were replaced with ones holding two or more people. Rule breaking became common, and in response more guards were hired, which increased costs. In turn, to contain costs, prison authorities brought in systems of contract labor. A manufacturer would supply the raw materials, and inmates were forced to produce a prescribed number of products within a set period of time. The prison received a portion of the proceeds from the sale of the goods to defray the costs of guard salaries and inmate food. The hope was that forced labor would eventually not only cover costs but also generate profits. That spelled the end of rules concerning silence and solitary work, as well as the educational intentions those rules had been intended to advance.

As work requirements increased, so did prisoner resistance in the form of refusals to work. In response, prison authorities turned to corporal punishment, isolation on very limited bread and water, and military-style rules. Recalcitrant prisoners were beaten, strung up by their thumbs, or dunked in ice water, and then forced to return to work. Treatment became more strictly regimented, with prisoners being lined up when leaving their cells to go to the workshops and required to place a hand on the shoulder of the man in front as they marched forward in "lockstep." Upon arrival, prisoners also now had their heads shaved and were forced to don striped prison uniforms.

The similarities between forced labor in a prison and slavery did not go unremarked. Workingmen in the northern states in particular protested against contract labor as a tool of punishment. Their opposition sprang not merely from humanitarian sentiments; self-interest was also involved. Workingmen viewed prison labor as unfair competition, taking jobs away from upstanding citizens. But they also recognized that forced labor undermined democratic principles. The editor of one of the small workingmen's newspapers went so far as to advocate that improvements in the social conditions that led people to commit crimes should be pursued as a means to do away with the threat to jobs from contract labor. He editorialized that "the proper way to get rid of the evil of convict labor in competition with that of honest mechanics would be to remove the causes which produce convicts; to prevent *poverty* and *ignorance*." Despite such protests, when slavery was officially abolished in all of the states by passage of the Thirteenth Amendment in 1865, "involuntary servitude" for those being punished for commission of a crime was legally sanctioned, and that language remains in the Constitution to this day.

New arguments for prison reform gained traction after the Civil War. As peace returned to the divided nation, many reform societies and associations were formed to address social problems exacerbated by rapidly advancing industrialism and urbanization. One of these was the National Prison Association, founded in 1870. Numerous visitors to penitentiaries had reported that they were disorderly, dirty, and congested, a far cry from the places of silent work and personal reformation they were intended to be. As a corrective, reformers advocated formal programs of education to breathe new life into the belief that imprisonment could encourage individual transformation.

In their greater emphasis on education-oriented activities, the reformers were guided by an influential 1867 report written for the Prison Association of New York by Enoch Cobb Wines, a one-time schoolmaster turned Congregational minister, and Theodore Dwight, another former schoolmaster, who became a lawyer and founding dean of the Columbia Law School. No penitentiary, the report stated, was meeting expectations to advance "the reformation of its subjects and their restoration to civil life as honest and industrious citizens." The authors recommended that "the law of love" replace "the law of force" in prisons. Prisoners should be allowed opportunities for supervised socializing as well as for literacy instruction and Bible study in Sunday schools and for independent reading. Prison libraries should be created. "A penal establishment," the report maintained, "should be, as it were, one vast school, in which almost everything is made subservient to instruction in some form or other—mental, moral, religious or industrial."[10]

Soon after the report was published, a large national congress on prison reform was convened in Cincinnati, Ohio, where Zebulon Reed Brockway delivered the "most able" of all the papers.[11] Born in Lyme, Connecticut, in 1827, Brockway was the son of a commissioner of the Connecticut state prison. After visiting the prison with his father as a child, he decided to devote himself to prison work, and his long career began with a job as a guard in Wethersfield, Connecticut. From there he moved through a number of increasingly responsible positions, and in 1861 he was appointed superintendent of the penitentiary in Detroit, Michigan. While there, he experimented with giving inmates privileges in exchange for good behavior and with education as a means of preparing people for release. His work in Detroit led to the invitation to speak at the Cincinnati conference, and his speech, in turn, led to his appointment as superintendent of New York State's first reformatory. That facility in Elmira, New York, opened in 1876, and it was there that Brockway developed a program to implement the ideas he had discussed at the Cincinnati meeting.

Upon admission, inmates, all of whom were first-time offenders between sixteen and thirty years old, were assessed to determine their need for reformation. New York State law mandated that each man serve a six-year sentence, but Brockway advocated for a new system, whereby prisoners would be given marks for their performance in reformatory classes, with high performers being eligible for supervised release before their terms were up. Known as parole, this new system began to operate after passage of the New York State Indeterminate Sentence Act of 1877. Approval of early release was the responsibility of a board of managers, relying on clear guidelines: six months of perfect marks led to extra privileges, and another six months of perfect marks made one eligible for parole; bad marks led to restrictions of privileges, with those with the worst records being required to wear red suits, walk in lockstep with other prisoners whenever leaving their cells, and forgo all correspondence and visiting privileges.

In addition, all Elmira prisoners were forced to go to chapel regularly, to spend a certain amount of time reading in a well-stocked library, and to attend the prison school, which was presided over by a professor from nearby Elmira College, with some of the more educated inmates acting as instructors. Reading, writing, arithmetic, geography, the natural sciences, bookkeeping, and physiology were taught, and training in thirty-four different trades was offered. To round out the program, lectures were offered on Sundays by volunteer visitors, and extracurricular activities were organized, including publication of a prison newspaper and sports, such as baseball and football.

According to an official history of Elmira, the courses offered in the education program were considered "treatments" integral to the mandated regime of reformation. However, because they were required, the men reportedly resented them.[12] While Brockway had hoped that indeterminate sentencing would increase motivation to cooperate with the reformatory's goals, the paternalistic control that was imposed instead provoked resistance.

Other familiar problems further undermined Brockway's aspirations almost from the start. Judges sent new inmates to Elmira faster than current inmates could be paroled, which resulted in overcrowding. Many were older than the anticipated age and were repeat offenders, and they were more willing to fight institutional demands. As discipline declined, harsh punishment increased, which, in turn, evoked more inmate resistance in the form of fights, escapes, and collective revolts. Lacking sufficient staff, Brockway appointed some inmates to be "monitors," who were allowed to employ corporal punishments, which further intensified tensions. The system of parole was another source of trouble. Both prison managers and inmates complained that parole officers received little training and sometimes returned former inmates to prison for reasons as frivolous as using tobacco.

Although Brockway was lauded for a time as a pioneer of modern penology, he retired in 1900 under a cloud cast by charges of mistreatment and prison corruption. He had, in fact, exhibited a sadistic streak, admitting to personally whipping and punching inmates and chaining them in solitary confinement—then called "rest cures"—for months at a time on only bread and water. He was proud of what he called "scientific whipping," which required that the person doing the whipping be in such control of himself that every lash was administered with the same force as the last and the next. Such techniques, he told his critics, were necessary because some of the men sent to Elmira were "creatures of instinct" who needed to have their conduct "promptly arrested."[13] However "benevolent" the educational aims of the new reformatory may have been, the reality was that recalcitrant prisoners faced repression of the harshest sort.

In spite of the shortcomings at Elmira, the emphasis on education pioneered there had wide influence. It inspired Josephine Shaw Lowell, the first woman commissioner of the State Board of Charities, and Abby Hopper Gibbons, president of the Women's Prison Association, to demand that the New York State legislature establish a reformatory for young women convicted of misdemeanors. Previously, women had been held in separate rooms or wings within prisons for men and were offered very few rehabilitative activities. At the penitentiary in Auburn, New York, for example, women were placed in an overcrowded, unventilated attic, not allowed outside, and given nothing to do but sew. A chaplain there observed in 1830 that "to be a male convict in this prison would be quite tolerable, but to be a *female* convict, for any protracted period, would be worse than death."[14] The circumstances for women at Auburn were typical.

To develop a better model, reformers secured support to open the Hudson House of Refuge for Women in 1887, in Hudson, New York, followed in 1893 by a similar institution in Albion and in 1901 by one at Bedford Hills. Katherine Bement Davis became the first superintendent at Bedford Hills and remained at the helm for the institution's first thirteen years. A Rochester native, she was an alumna of Vassar College, with a doctorate in economics from the University of Chicago and experience as head resident of a settlement house in Philadelphia. She insisted that the institution be run "as a school and not a prison," and therefore adopted the cottage plan of living, invented at the Lancaster Industrial School for Girls in Massachusetts, the first reform school for girls, opened in 1856.[15] The grounds looked much like those of a small private college, with the women housed in comfortable cottages dispersed around the larger administration building, rather than in large dormitories or cell blocks.[16] She also relied on "mental tests," just then being invented by psychologists, to separate out "the feeble minded," who, she believed, could not benefit from Bedford Hills' education programs and should therefore be incarcerated indefinitely.[17]

The Elmira model also led to the introduction of more education into prisons for men in much of the United States, with more and more wardens beginning to view the industrial work as analogous to classes in a trade school. The classification of new arrivals according to what was deemed to be their need for rehabilitation also became more common, as did the practice of allowing men in the top category opportunities to participate in academic classes, organize literary societies, and hold social activities in the evening. By the turn of the century, indeterminate sentences and parole were becoming standard, with marks for academic work or vocational training counting toward release. The notable exception was in the South, where punishment remained the goal and forced labor in mines and farms, often under horrific conditions, was common.

Brockway's innovations also mobilized a new generation of penal reformers, among whom Thomas Mott Osborne was the most prominent. He instituted a pioneering system of prisoner self-government at two New York State prisons, Auburn and Sing Sing. The new system Osborne implemented sheds light on why so many education programs, though increasingly popular with prison authorities, commonly provoked resentment among the people they were meant to help.

Osborne was born into a family of reformers. There were many prominent abolitionists and advocates of women's rights among his relatives, including Lucretia Coffin Mott, who helped organize the 1848 Seneca Falls Convention, where the first declaration of women's rights was promulgated. Before he began his career as a prison reformer, Osborne had been active in local politics, serving two terms as mayor of Auburn as well as participating in other civic and benevolent causes. After reading a book entitled *My Life in Prison* by a former inmate at San Quentin, Osborne turned his attention to prisons and prevailed upon Governor William Sulzer to appoint him chairman of the New York State Prison Reform Commission.

That appointment enabled Osborne to gain permission to be locked up in the Auburn Penitentiary for six days as "Tom Brown, Inmate 33,333X." He claimed that he did this because he wanted to see for himself what criminals were like rather than trust descriptions written by others. "'The Criminal,'" he said, "has been extensively studied, and deductions as to his instincts, habits and character drawn from the measurement of his ears and nose; but I wanted to get acquainted with the man himself, the man behind the statistics."[18] Subsequently, in the style of contemporary muckrakers, he spoke out at reform meetings and in essays published in newspapers, magazines, and books about his experiences at Auburn. He described the horrible food, the cruelty of some of the guards, the petty rules that governed every aspect of one's life, and, on the other side, the humanity and intelligence of his fellow prisoners. The criminal "differs less than the layman thinks from the ordinary run of humanity," he insisted. Imprisonment was nothing less than "cruel slavery," he maintained, and he condemned "the bitterness of solitary."[19]

The experience shaped the reforms Osborne sought to institute, first at the Auburn prison, and then at Sing Sing, where he became warden in 1914. While imprisoned as Tom Brown, Osborne got to know an inmate who suggested that he set up a "Good Conduct League" to oversee a self-government plan. The suggestion hit home, reminding Osborne of his experience serving earlier as a trustee of a student-run reform school. As a consequence, he convinced the warden of Auburn to allow him to work with the men held there to establish a Mutual Welfare League within the prison.

Two men from each of the prison's industrial shops were elected to a board of delegates, which established the rules and routines for the prison, under Osborne's forceful guidance. He thought that prisons should be understood as education facilities, and he told the men that the rules and regulations were to reflect friendly relationships between guards and the men they supervised, "exactly as in any school." This meant, he explained, that just as teachers and students shared a common wish that students learn, the guards and prisoners should also share that goal. He objected to "the false view of the teacher and the false view of the scholar," explaining that "the false view of the teacher is that he must emphasize his authority from above; the false view of the scholar is that as long as he is under tyrannical authority the scholars must band together against the teacher."[20] If prisoners governed themselves, he argued, that adversarial relationship would not prevail.

With that in mind, Osborne encouraged the board of delegates to appoint committees from among the men to manage everything from sanitation to the reception area for visitors and the organization of work. In lieu of the previous system of severe prison discipline imposed from above, he proposed an inmate court to function as a social ethics class in which the men discussed what was right and wrong about everyday occurrences in the prison.

After the board of delegates had finished their plan, the entire prison population was asked to ratify it. Osborne presented the plan to all of the fourteen hundred men then held at Auburn. "You are either going to be ruled by Arbitrary Power, or else you are going to rule yourself and assist those whom you select" to serve as police, he told the assembled company. "In other words, are you going to be held as slaves, or are you going to be treated as men?

You must take the responsibility of men and one of these responsibilities consists in seeing that the rest of you, that every one of
you sees that the other behaves."[21] Although men expressed many
worries about matters such as who would have supervisory powers
and under what circumstances, the plan was eventually ratified via
a unanimous vote.[22]

Contemporaries said that the Mutual Welfare League worked
quite well at Auburn. Even the officers were enthusiastic in endors-
ing it. Because the men could exercise more control over their lives,
the plan helped diminish hostility between the men in custody and
those who supervised them. After the launching of the league, less
violence broke out. A decrease in mental health problems was also
reported, and drug traffic was significantly reduced. In addition,
the men took advantage of opportunities to organize events, sometimes putting on concerts and receptions for the officers and visitors. "Alumni," as those released were often called, returned for
reunions and held fund-raisers to support projects initiated by the
men. They also organized forums to discuss "the new penology."

Later, at Sing Sing, where Osborne served as warden from 1914
to 1916, he promoted the Golden Rule Brotherhood, a replica of
the Auburn prisoners' association. As at Auburn, the results were
said to be positive. According to an admiring biographer of Osborne, Sing Sing "took on the aspect of a community, of a school.
The men themselves began to talk about it as 'the college for the
remaking of men.' Some called it the 'University of Sing Sing.'"[23]

It is difficult to know how well the reforms Osborne instituted
at Auburn and Sing Sing actually embodied his ideals. As historian
Rebecca M. McLennan has argued in a detailed analysis of Osborne's experiment with prison self-government, there was more
top-down management involved at both prisons than Osborne was
inclined to mention. Prison authorities never fully ceded control of
either prison, and, owing to fears of retribution, the men who were
in custody were never fully free to say what they thought about

Osborne and his ideas. That notwithstanding, Osborne's experiment demonstrated the power of even small degrees of freedom to promote more cooperative behavior among prisoners and better order in prisons. As Osborne repeatedly explained, he was less interested in the reformation of the men than in showing that coercion could be replaced with freedom and shame with dignity. Providing for these, he argued, would inspire men to take responsibility on their own initiative for pursuing a law-abiding life after release. "Outside the walls a man must choose between work and idleness, between honesty and crime," he observed in a 1904 address. "Why not let him teach himself these lessons before he goes out?"[24]

Many of Osborne's contemporaries thought he was coddling the inmates. Longtime FBI director J. Edgar Hoover, for one, dubbed his kind of approach "cream puff" criminology.[25] Critics did not share the belief that underpinned Osborne's thinking that changes in one's environment could result in changes in behavior. They asserted instead that criminals were innately depraved. Osborne became a target of frequent criticism in the press. During his tenure at Sing Sing, reporters constantly wrote about alleged mismanagement, and ultimately Osborne was indicted on a number of criminal charges, including having sex with the men. He was acquitted and returned to his post at the prison, but soon thereafter he decided that the constant battle to carry out his ideas was not worth the fight, and he retired.

Although the prison self-government organization did not long survive his departure, Osborne's ideas inspired a generation of younger penal reformers, the most important of whom was Austin MacCormick. Throughout a long and distinguished career in criminology and prison administration, MacCormick advised many state and federal commissions on prison reform and held leadership positions in both the federal prison system and the New York City Department of Corrections. His most important achievement may have been designing a system of reformatories for New York State, which became a model of progressive penology. Like Osborne, MacCormick believed "the criminal was 'just like us'" and was convinced that prisons could and should be sites of "self-transformation" through opportunities for education and participation in prison governance. He hoped that education could counter the harm caused by the boredom and cruelty of life in prison.[26] These beliefs guided his planning for the reformatory system.

MacCormick recommended that all prisoners be assessed and classified, with hard-core criminals separated from those he believed became involved in crime as a result of unemployment, which he assumed was due to "vocational incompetence." The former group should be housed in "big house" maximum-security prisons, the latter group in minimum-security reformatories, with rich education offerings geared to inmates' interests. Rather than viewing labor simply as a means of keeping inmates busy, MacCormick insisted that prison work should be designed as an educational activity, which could both socialize inmates into working life and help them understand the importance of their labor to everyone in society. This was meant to ensure that the prisoners became dissatisfied "with their former mode of living" and would henceforth willingly conform to society's laws and social expectations, especially with expectations to work.[27]

Possibly because it was mandated, MacCormick's efforts to replace more punitive approaches with ones based on "social education" were not entirely successful. University of Florida historian Joseph Spillane has documented the problems that emerged at Coxsackie prison, one of the reformatories where MacCormick's ideas were tried out, and similar problems were reported at the other reformatories, with conditions in the reformatories described as akin to a state of "ceaseless war."[28] According to Spillane, the educators the reformatories employed were often at odds with the security personnel, wanting time and space for their classes that interfered with normal prison routines. MacCormick and his colleagues secured financing to establish a Central Guard School, to teach the officers to respect their charges. It seems clear, however, that even after their nine-week residencies, those overseeing the prisons did not adopt the belief that criminals were just like noncriminals, only lacking in sufficient socialization. According to one man held at Coxsackie, the officers "use lumber to educate you when you step out of line. . . . Coming from Brooklyn I have a bad habit of saying 'yeah' in response to a question. . . . When a so-called correctional guard asked me a question, and I said 'yeah' . . . he hit me in the face with a bat, and I had to have most of my teeth taken out. So that started my introduction to 'rehabilitation,' at the end of this stick."[29]

Antagonism between guards and the men they oversaw intensified with time. Beginning in the 1920s, counseling programs based on the latest studies in psychology and psychiatry came into operation, but these were apparently ineffective in changing behavior. Beginning in the 1940s, the arrival of greater numbers of young inmates at the reformatories, many of whom were gang members, or who joined gangs once inside, did not help. Gang assaults among inmates became frequent, as did sexual and racial violence. Drugs were widely available and, beginning in the late 1940s, as heroin addiction became more common among high school–aged New Yorkers, increasing numbers of addicts found their way to Coxsackie or one of the other reformatories. By 1951, 22 percent of the men arriving at the reformatories were heroin users.[30]

Racial segregation was practiced at Coxsackie and added to the tensions. Spillane believes white officers encouraged this.[31] He includes many accounts by men in custody there who described the manifestations of racism. One young man, named John Mack, got into a fight with a man who had called him nigger. When Mack was taken to the warden, the warden apparently screamed at him, saying, "You're a nigger, nigger, NIGGER." Mack commented that he had never "seen such an open, naked, official hatred before."[32] In Spillane's account, white prisoners had more privileges and better job assignments than blacks, which further increased hostility. By 1952, the problems had become so bad at the reformatories that one of them was designated as an end-of-the-line institution, used to hold men who were too difficult to handle in the other facilities. Strikes and riots began breaking out.

The tensions at Coxsackie became common in prisons around the country. One way that African Americans responded was by converting to Islam, which helped strengthen solidarity among converts, who defined themselves as members of a separate, self-defined community. During the late 1960s, more inmates also joined the Black Panther Party to demonstrate their independence from and hostility toward white prison officials.

Tensions became particularly intense in California, where the wartime defense industries had served as a magnet for African Americans searching for good jobs. As the black population of the state increased, so did the black population of the prisons. While blacks made up 20.7 percent of the San Quentin population in 1951, by 1980 they comprised 36.6 percent.[33] As Eric Cummins has pointed out in *The Rise and Fall of California's Radical Prison Movement*, blacks were pitted against white authorities at every stage of involvement with the criminal justice system, from arrest, conviction, sentencing, and classification upon arrival at a prison, all the way through to parole hearings. He believes that their resentment of white racism fueled increasing resistance to all aspects of their confinement.

Within this racially charged atmosphere, efforts to rehabilitate and educate were sometimes turned to purposes other than those that were intended. One program, called bibliotherapy, which was introduced into California prisons in the 1950s, was intended to promote resocialization through reading and writing, with an emphasis on "great works" of literature. Though the "therapeutic" intent of the program was ridiculed by both prison officials and inmates, one ironic effect was that is seemed to spark a dramatic increase in writing by the incarcerated, much of it about life inside the prison system.[34] When some of this work reached the general public, it became influential in building support for prisoner rights advocacy among both black and white civil rights activists.[35] Black Panther Eldridge Cleaver's *Soul on Ice*, first published as an essay in *Ramparts* magazine and then, in 1968, in book form, told of Cleaver's personal evolution from drug dealing to revolutionary politics, in the process commenting on topics ranging from American foreign policy to love between black men and white women. In *Soledad Brothers* (1970), another Black Panther, George Jackson, expressed his rage at the oppressive workings of the white capitalist system and its prison systems. The book was named by the *New York Times* as one of the ten best books of the year and won wide acclaim and a large readership.

Protests against the brutality of prison guards and the conditions that prevailed in many facilities also became more frequent, leading to increasing riots, the most prolonged of which occurred at Attica prison in upstate New York in 1971. That riot was heavily covered in the news and was especially alarming because ten guards and twenty-one inmates were killed and eighty-nine more were seriously injured. After Attica, critics on both the left and right side of the political spectrum repudiated the rehabilitative ideal championed by MacCormick and Osborne. On the left, the focus was on the injustice of imposing "treatments" on prisoners, while on the right, the violence and protests seemed to provide strong evidence that education and rehabilitative programs were ineffective, if not counterproductive.

This was the political situation that led to the commissioning of the Martinson Report. The New York State Department of Corrections requested funds to investigate whether there was any evidence that prison education programs were worth the state's investment of tax funds. To find out, the legislature authorized a multiyear study, running from 1966 until 1969, to be conducted by a five-member professional staff, supplemented by five expert consultants. One of the consultants hired was Robert Martinson, then working as a criminology professor at the University of California, Berkeley.

The overwhelming acceptance of the claim that "nothing works" to reduce recidivism can be attributed largely to the confluence of criticism on both the left and the right. As historian David Rothman commented in *The Nation* magazine in an article published in the wake of Martinson's *Public Interest* piece, there was "a startlingly unanimous view: incarceration has failed."[36] Political scientist James Q. Wilson of Harvard University, an influential conservative voice in the study of the criminal justice system, went so far as to argue in his 1975 book *Thinking About Crime* (and the many prior essays on which it was based) that only dreamers would insist on trying to limit crime by transforming criminals. That was not possible. Instead, Wilson insisted, incentives should be changed, with punishment becoming ever more strict and immediate.

Martinson had pointed out in his *Public Interest* article that many of the studies examined were flawed and had clearly suggested that better research was needed. But his ultimate conclusion, that there was "very little reason to hope that we have in fact found a sure way of reducing recidivism through rehabilitation," swayed both expert and public opinion. "Nothing works" became, as one commentator aptly phrased it, "a slogan for the times."[37] Any more nuanced arguments Martinson may have wished to present were lost in the pessimism.

Five years after his *Public Interest* article appeared, Martinson published a retraction in the *Hofstra Law Review*. Based on further research as well as a more careful analysis of the statistical assessment by which the causal link between programs and recidivism was measured for the report—which he found to be flawed—he was convinced, he explained, that "contrary to my previous position, some treatment programs *do* have an appreciable effect on recidivism." For that reason, he continued, he not only withdrew his previous conclusion, but also "protested at the slogan used by the media to sum up what I said—'nothing works.'"[38] Subsequent research confirmed his new perspective, but Martinson's retraction was too little, too late. Whereas the *Public Interest* article was very widely read and quoted, the one in the *Hofstra Law Review* was largely ignored.

Support for scaling back education and other programs aimed at reducing recidivism grew, and over the course of the subsequent decades more and more such activities were discontinued. Meanwhile, the Supreme Court repudiated the idea that prison sentences should be tied to efforts to "rehabilitate" offenders. In 1989, in the case of *Mistretta v. United States*, the court ruled that possibilities for rehabilitation should not be taken into account in any way in sentencing decisions. Martinson never learned the full extent of the influence of his *Public Interest* article. In 1980, he committed suicide by jumping out of his apartment window in New York City.

Of course, Martinson's article alone did not cause the ensuing decades' shift toward punishment and the social isolation of prisoners. As new laws led to mass incarceration and increasing numbers of African Americans were sent to prison, a more punitive approach to imprisonment gained traction as part of the migration of "Dixie-style" prison management out of the South. In his remarkable study of prisons, *Texas Tough: The Rise of America's Prison Empire*, historian Robert Perkinson of the University of Hawaii at Manoa asserts that the aim was to re-create the bondage that had dominated southern penitentiaries and prison farms.[39] Of course, economics also played a part—as more money was needed for building prisons, funding for prison education (and education more generally) lost out; racism was also a factor.

Today, the pendulum is swinging back. Support for education

in prison is growing, thanks to concerns about the multifaceted costs of mass incarceration as well as solid evidence attesting to the positive impact education in prison can have. As new programs are developed and approved, it is vital that advocates heed the lessons of history about how education should be offered, if it is to be effective. Imposing education programs tends to evoke resentment among the incarcerated. But opportunities for education are likely to be embraced when choice and self-direction are involved. Education should not be forced on people in prison, nor considered or presented as part of a punishment regime. Creating conditions of freedom within institutions designed to remove freedom is a difficult challenge, but it is a challenge that can and must be met.

7

What Works?

Insights from the Bard Prison Initiative

When I first became involved in the Bard Prison Initiative, I was startled to hear the students I was teaching talk about coming to class as "coming to Bard." We were sitting in a room within a maximum-security prison with windows that could not be opened more than an inch or two. Yet they were speaking as though they had been transported to Bard's main campus in Annandale-on-Hudson, New York. Now after many years of teaching and advising in the prisons, I understand what they meant. Those of us who are involved in Bard's prison program regard each of the six sites where courses are offered as another one of Bard's many, far-flung campuses. When students step over the threshold into a Bard class or study room, they know Bard norms will apply. They are regarded as students, and their status as prisoners is irrelevant. Though students sometimes choose to tell a faculty member why they are in prison, faculty members never ask them what their crimes were. They are treated in exactly the same manner as all other Bard College students and held to exactly the same standards. Students are expected to act respectfully to one another as well as to faculty members, but vigorous debate and disagreement are encouraged, including with faculty members. In speaking of "coming to Bard" students are referring to the fact that "in Bard" academic values govern and they may think, speak, and act as free men and women.

Of course, prison rules and regulations are still in force. The program is possible only because the New York State Department of Corrections and Community Supervision has sanctioned it and reviews all educational materials before they are taken into a prison. Faculty must be approved by the department, as well as photographed and fingerprinted. In addition, they must undergo standard departmental training, consisting of watching and discussing a video about how to avoid problems. They must also abide by dress regulations—no blue jeans and nothing that is the same green as the uniforms—and they go through a metal detector upon entering the facilities and are not permitted to bring cell phones inside.

Founded in 1999 (though it did not become a degree-granting program until 2001), the Bard Prison Initiative enrolls three hundred full-time students, spread across six New York State correctional facilities, five for men, three of which are maximum security and two of which are medium security; and one for women, a medium-security facility. Admission to the college is highly selective, with all students entering on a track toward an associate's degree. Those who do well at the associate's degree level may apply for admission to the bachelor's degree track, which enrolls many fewer students. All students pursuing the bachelor's degree are housed at the Eastern Correctional Facility in Napanoch, New York, which is the hub of the college, with the most students and classes, as well as the richest array of lectures, concerts, and other extracurricular offerings, and which contains classrooms, a Bard library, and two special study rooms equipped with computer terminals hosting many of the items available electronically through the Bard library but without connections to the Internet. The two other maximum-security facilities are, in a sense, "feeder" programs, where students begin associate's degrees that are usually finished at Eastern; the two medium-security facilities are places where men are sent by the Department of Corrections and Community Supervision when they are five years or less away from release and often after they have finished their Bard degrees. Unfortunately, since all the work for the bachelor's degree is offered in a prison for men, women cannot get a bachelor's through Bard's prison program, although, if admitted, they can continue on to a bachelor's degree at Bard's main campus in Annandale after release.

This relatively large and comprehensive program operates entirely on private money, raised through constant fund-raising from generous individuals and a few philanthropic foundations. Its budget of $2.7 million a year covers modest stipends for the faculty; all books and other educational materials, including everything from computers to tapes for foreign language instruction; and the expenses involved in operating a reentry program for the 360 alums who are now home and living in or near New York City.

In designing the college program, Bard has created the conditions that history has shown are most conducive to deep and lasting learning. Students are invited to enroll, rather than mandated to attend, and once they are admitted, they have considerable freedom in choosing classes, majors, and thesis topics. I believe the sense of freedom and independence students feel "in Bard" is crucial to the success of the program, as is the unusual rigor of the academic program along with the respect for intellect that this nurtures.

Bard's success can be measured in many ways. The most often cited yardstick is the greatly reduced recidivism rate of students. In essence, men and women who have been enrolled in or graduated from Bard do not return to prison. As already noted, among those who have done some course work but gone home before completing a degree, the return rate is 5 percent, while among degree holders it is 2 percent. By stark contrast, the average return rate nationally is about 50 percent. The course work is not the only factor contributing to this result. Upon release, alums receive assistance with the challenges of returning home, including help in finding housing, health care, and work. But the students report that the quality of the education they have received is the deciding factor in their ability to be successful after going home. Of course, it is also the case that men and women who choose to apply to Bard tend to be individuals who are already searching for ways to prepare for a new life after release. They are probably not the individuals who are most likely to recidivate. That said, according to their own reports, it is going to college that enables them to turn the corner.

Another indicator of the program's success is that many students succeed after release in securing further education, either completing a bachelor's degree or moving on to a master's or doctorate. A few earn master's degrees from the New York Theological Seminary while still incarcerated; this is the only such degree available in New York State. The college experience can kindle an ongoing interest in learning. Many students have also demonstrated a continuing commitment to Bard itself, with most alums contributing financially, some sending modest checks even as they stretch to pay for graduate school. Alums also generally respond to any request Bard makes of them, to help a peer just arriving home, to meet with potential donors, or even to sit for interviews about their experience for a news story or a book, including this one, or for a Ken Burns documentary projected for release in 2018. The many positive spillover effects for the students' families and communities, as they graduate, find good jobs and contribute to their family's financial support, pay taxes, and work on neighborhood projects, also testify to the powerful impact Bard has on its students.

The students have much to say about what makes the program so effective in developing their talents and confidence and inspiring ambition. Many stress the importance of the autonomy they are offered as the primary factor. They report feeling a sense of freedom and independence in being Bard students. The demands of the curriculum come in as a close second factor. The high standards require full attention and convey to students that they are getting the "real thing," not some watered-down version of a college curriculum. Students report that classes are "totally absorbing," which is clearly evident in the classrooms. The intensity of student engagement is seen in the consistently lively class discussions. The study rooms are always full. In one-on-one conversations with faculty, students often report having read several more books than the ones assigned in order to investigate the topics at hand more deeply. They regularly ask for comments on essays they have written not for class, but just to express their views about someone running for office or an event in the news. On occasion, they buttonhole professors to talk about some particularly challenging philosophical puzzle they have been contemplating, such as how one knows what is and is not fair. Others have wanted to discuss an idea they have for a book they want to write or an organization they hope to establish once they are home.

Many students have said that they like being asked to push themselves and enjoy engaging in hard work. One student commented that if he had known "how *insane* the demands of the college are" he probably would not have applied, and then quickly added, "You know that's not really true. But the college does push you to the limit." Another student described his initial years in the college as "a trial by fire. You just had to learn and figure it out. You had no time for bullshit. You were fully absorbed—that felt good. Bard consumed my whole day." The high expectations convey strong confidence in the students' abilities, which many point to as an important factor in coming to believe they can meet the demands made of them.

Students often regard Bard's high standards as a common challenge that is shared across all members of a class. They emphasize that, while pushing them very hard, the Bard program promotes community and camaraderie among students rather than showmanship and competition. This is demonstrated by the support students offer each other, often studying in groups and tutoring those who are struggling. Some alums who have not yet been released also teach informal classes to help prepare those who want to enter the program. There is a determination to ensure that no one fails. The combination of being pushed to the limit and having a strong support network seems to encourage and sustain the deep engagement that effective education requires.

Students are aware before enrolling that the program will be an all-out challenge. That is conveyed in part by the fact that the program is highly selective, which is true both statistically, in that many more people apply than can be admitted, with the ratio sometimes being as high as ten to one, as well as in terms of the difficulty of the application process. Other college-in-prison programs that are selective also have high applicant-to-admission ratios, and those programs that admit students on a first-come, first-served basis, notably the Prison University Project at San Quentin, have long waiting lists. But Bard is definitely on the high-intensity side of the spectrum in terms of the time, energy, and care that is put into selection. As noted earlier, incarcerated students enter Bard on the associate's degree track; those who wish to continue and based on their academic achievement to date are permitted to do so must reapply. Ideally, twenty to thirty students will be admitted at the largest Bard sites, although that number is not absolute and classes vary in size across the six prisons.

All initial applicants must sit for an essay examination, which is given only once a year, in the summer. The exam is administered at each of the six prisons where Bard operates. Applicants have roughly two hours—"one mod" in prison language—to respond to one of three "prompts," which are generally passages from literature or news coverage. The prompts are varied in genre and students are free to write about whichever prompt they want. A prompt might be a paragraph from the Federalist Papers, a poem, or a passage from a recent work in the social sciences. One year, one of them was a selection from the poem "Touch Me," by Stanley Kunitz, which begins: "Summer is late, my heart . . ." Another was a passage from Alexis de Tocqueville's *Democracy in America* (1835): "Democracy makes every man forget his ancestors, but it hides descendants and separates his contemporaries from him." One exam prompt included a whole editorial column from the *New York Times*, which began: "It seems that every week a new book or major newspaper article appears showing that irrational decision-making helped cause the housing bubble or the rise in health care costs." No guidance is given about what to write in response to the prompts; no questions are asked and no explanations are offered as to what sorts of responses are expected. Some applicants write a paragraph, while others write several pages. Some applicants leave the exam room after thirty minutes, while others are still writing when the bell rings indicating it is time to head to their cells for the count.

Four or five faculty or staff members sit around a table in an office at the Annandale-on-Hudson campus to evaluate the essays. The range of accomplishment displayed in their writings makes the great leap in skills that will be demanded of students readily apparent. Although applicants must have at least completed a GED to apply to Bard, only a minority of them graduated from high school before being sent to prison, and some are not native speakers of English. Most of their writing is extremely weak, with few complete sentences and terrible spelling. Words must often be sounded out in order to grasp the author's intention. The spelling tends to be phonetic and is sometimes far off the mark, such as "rejewjinate" in place of "rejuvenate." Most of the essays are written in pencil, and the handwriting is often difficult to read.

Every year, some of the essays nevertheless clearly convey lively curiosity as well as ambition and a determination to succeed. Those are flagged and the applicants move on to the next step in the admission process. A passage like this would likely catch someone's eye: "I want to be like my grandfather because he read a lot of books and was able to tell what they said. That made him wise and everyone asked for his advice and respected him. I want to *work for respect*." Another passage likely to get a nod of approval is: "If I were Barrack Obama [sic], I would do more for poor men in New York and other citys. I would not deny my blackness." So would this line: "I want to go to college to show my son I can do it." Sometimes, particularly in response to prompts that touch on historical topics, applicants write that they want to study specific subjects in history, such as slavery, or the meaning of citizenship, constitutional law, or educational problems in inner cities. On occasion, essays relate that an applicant worked to prepare him- or herself for the admission exam. One applicant wrote that he had snuck off into a corner of the law library, when he was meant to be shelving books, to study a grammar manual he had found. Others have stated that they sought out already enrolled Bard students for advice about how to improve their writing before taking the test.

To identify those students who will move on to the next step, readers sometimes must grade several hundred essays. They first evaluate the essays independently, rating them five for the highest, and one for the lowest. They then compare their assessments, and this usually involves a good deal of disagreement and discussion on the way to consensus. Up to forty or so applicants per prison can be chosen for the next step of the process, which is an interview. Given the rigidity of prison schedules, the interviews must be brief, just ten or fifteen minutes, and conducted in rapid succession. Two faculty or staff members conduct each interview together. They ask applicants about their essays and about their reasons for wanting to go to college and try to assess an applicant's determination and drive. Hopefully those qualities will foster the persistence needed to surmount the high hurdles succeeding in college will involve. Interviewers work hard not to be unduly charmed by the most confident candidates or put off by those who are shy. Most applicants appear quite nervous, which is not surprising. The stakes are high; if applicants do not win a seat "in Bard," there is usually no alternative college to which they can apply. They can, however, reapply to Bard the next year, and many do, with some having applied as many as eight times before gaining entrance.

After the interviews, the faculty and staff who have been involved compare impressions and conduct a form of triage, trying to select those with the most promise. Students who are repeat applicants will likely have an edge, especially if, between application cycles, they have engaged in serious reading or grammar study, borrowing books from the prison library or from a peer, or enrolling in one of the preparatory classes run by Bard alums not yet released. The main criteria in selection are intellectual hunger, realistic expectations of having to do hard work, and determination to succeed.

Given the difficulty of the process and the odds of admission, applying is a courageous act. Doing so risks embarrassment among peers, since word about who has sat for the entrance exam, who made it to the interview, and who was not admitted spreads throughout the facilities. In addition, students have told me that some among the prison population disparage applying as acting "bourgeois" or "giving in to whitey." Standing up to that kind of peer pressure takes considerable strength. So does dealing with the pain of rejection.

Bard would not be the best college option for all who apply. While it is very unfortunate that alternatives are not available in most of the prisons where Bard operates, it would not make sense to admit students who do not appear able to rise to the academic challenges. The admission process is designed to identify those most likely to succeed, while also fulfilling a number of other purposes. First, intense selectivity enhances the value of admission in the eyes of the students, making acceptance a significant achievement in itself—a badge of honor. In this way the admission process further fuels the students' motivation. Selectivity also underscores that enrolling in the college is a privilege.

The admission process clearly communicates that this privilege is being offered to them as part of a social contract. For their part, students must work hard, often having to give up other activities to make more time for study. On occasion, students have even said that they have asked their families to stop visiting during a month when they are especially busy with papers and exams. Some have reported giving up a job that enabled them to earn money to buy things in the commissary. On the part of the faculty, there is a promise to regard each man or woman as a potentially promising student and to offer those who are admitted all that is needed to realize their potential at the highest possible level.

Intense selectivity serves at least one additional function. The questions asked during the interview can encourage students to begin to engage in metacognition, meaning thinking about how they think and the ways of thinking that are most likely to facilitate learning. Educators now generally believe that helping students develop metacognitive assessments of their own approaches to learning, in some cases shedding bad habits and in others trying out new strategies, can greatly enhance their capacity to interact effectively with the materials they are studying. One of the strengths of the Bard program is that it helps students learn *how to learn* and become highly self-reflective about their strengths and weaknesses in absorbing information and in organizing their studying. It encourages them to think constantly about what struggling with calculus, or German grammar, or Plato's *Republic* is doing for them, both as students and as people, and which approaches to the materials are more and less useful. In that way, the content of the curriculum, while important in itself, becomes instrumental in preparing them for continuing personal and intellectual growth.

The application process is even more rigorous for students continuing to the bachelor's degree program. The students who apply must complete regular Bard admission forms, submit their transcripts from the associate's program, and secure letters of recommendation from faculty members who know them well. Even more than being rejected for the associate's degree program, being turned down for the bachelor's program is a severe blow. While students can reapply for the associate's degree program, that is not true for the bachelor's program. This is not due to resource constraints. Rather, once students have a track record of academic accomplishment, the likelihood of those who struggled with associate-level work succeeding in higher-level classes is low, and a little more reading or grammar study is not likely to have a meaningful impact.

Of course, as indicated, only a relatively small segment of the students earning associate's degrees move on to the bachelor's. Nevertheless, all students admitted to the program face high standards throughout their period of study. Regardless of degree status, students must complete the copious homework assignments on time and show up to class ready to participate. We expect them to ask for help when they need it, seeking out faculty members or advisors as well as staff tutors and their peers. In return, the faculty is committed to ensuring that students succeed. Some students struggle, some do not do very well, and not everyone makes it into the bachelor's program, but almost no one has dropped out of the program and almost everyone has graduated. Those few who have left have generally done so because they were moved by the Department of Corrections and Community Supervision to another facility or were released.

The high standards maintained by Bard communicate that faculty members have confidence in the students' capacity to learn. Even those who have not always been good students are not written off as simply too "dumb" to go to college, and the students rise to the potential the faculty sees in them. The growth in students' competence is often quite astounding. They acquire new knowledge and additional skills quickly and well even though their prior educations have generally been limited and usually of poor quality. Many also come from families whose members could not model correctly spoken English or disciplined study habits, or otherwise facilitate school success. Others grew up in foster care or group homes where such guidance was entirely lacking.

Despite many of the students' weak academic preparation, Bard does not offer remedial instruction in basic language and math skills, typically characterized by practice exercises that focus on introducing rules via drill in subject-verb agreement, followed by sentence formation, and then constructing paragraphs, all taught with text that has little or no informational or literary value. Although Bard's prison program does stipulate that at least twelve of the sixty-six credits required for the associate's degree must be earned in entry-level grammar, composition, and math classes, the pedagogy does not rest on rote drill. Composition instruction, for example, combines the reading of classical, canonical texts, among them Plato's *Republic*, the *Iliad* and the *Odyssey*, Shakespeare's *King Lear*, Darwin's *On Natural Selection*, and novels such as Margaret Atwood's *Good Bones* and Virginia Woolf's *To the Lighthouse*. Throughout two semesters, students analyze these texts in class discussions and in weekly response papers. They are also required to write three longer essays presenting analyses and arguments about these texts, and then to rewrite each of the essays after a critique by the professor. Grammar instruction is included, involving traditional review of the parts of speech and parts of a sentence, paragraphing, and punctuation, using Strunk and White's classic *The Elements of Style*, along with a grammar manual. But the rules and style guidelines are introduced as part of discussion of thought-provoking, interesting literature.

All students receive the grammar manual that they use in these introductory classes as soon as they are notified of their admission. Doing so sends a message: the college will provide you with resources, but you are responsible for applying yourself to learn the basic skills that are required for success. The Bard philosophy is that students will be more inspired and will learn better when emphasis is placed on their own agency, requiring them to study on their own and to seek out assistance on their own terms, rather than imposing stultifying instruction on them. The result is that students study the grammar manuals intensively, often congregating in the yard to discuss them, with students helping one another master rules. The pages become more dog-eared over the years. Placing emphasis on student responsibility highlights again that they are being offered an opportunity, not being compelled to change, as was the case with the flawed approach of so many prison education programs in the past. Bard does not consider the education it provides in prisons to be a program of rehabilitation; rather, it is offering men and women who happen to be in prison an excellent college education. It is liberating minds, not judging or remediating them.

The Bard curriculum is that of a typical liberal arts college, including English literature, foreign language (currently, German and Chinese), philosophy, social sciences, history, mathematics, science, and the arts. All classes are small and usually taught in a seminar style, with in-class discussion, rather than lectures, predominating. Typically, first-year students are seated alongside students finishing their bachelor's degrees or even alums, who are eligible to take additional postdegree classes, while they serve out their sentences. As has been found in studies of inter-age grouping in K–12 education, this intermingling facilitates peer modeling, with the less advanced students observing and copying the behaviors of the more advanced ones. In discussions of what is effective about the approach, less advanced students often remark that they have learned from the way more advanced students ask questions in class or disagree with other students or the professor.

They say this helps them develop confidence about participating in the back-and-forth or asking questions. Particularly as new students discover how difficult classes are, they develop a new admiration for those who have preceded them. They pay keen attention to the ways in which their more experienced peers behave in class, the study room, and doubtless even in the yard. As for the more advanced students, they discuss "socializing" new students, often saying they are helping to "shape them up," teaching them to listen carefully to what other people have say, to respect people who have different opinions, to volunteer their own ideas but not to show off, and to take part in conversations without trying to dominate them.

Bard's prison program replicates the regular Bard College curriculum in all respects. Just as at the Annandale campus, all students begin with a "Workshop in Language and Thinking," which is an intensive introduction to the various genres of literature—poetry, essays, scientific reports—and different kinds of writing. All students must also enroll in "Citizen Science," which is a two-week class focusing on natural science and the scientific method. A recent iteration of this class dealt with infectious diseases in a global society. The class mixed readings from current media accounts about AIDS and Ebola with chapters from works in evolutionary theory, such as Charles Darwin's *The Descent of Man* and Richard Dawkins's *The Blind Watchmaker*. Bard also stipulates that all students fulfill requirements in quantitative analysis, the practice of art, introduction to the social sciences, regional diversity studies (about the cultures and histories of countries around the globe), and literature or analysis of the arts. In addition, all students must enroll in at least two elective classes that are writing intensive. These are regular content classes with a strong emphasis on drafting papers and revising them with a focus on both grammar and the substance of a student's argument. The electives offered are remarkably varied, including, as just a few recent examples, "Migration and Diaspora in Global Perspective," "Molecules, Cells, and

Organs," "The Irish in America," and "Rebels With(out) a Cause: Great Works in German Literature."

In planning the curriculum, the prison program seeks to offer a wide selection of classes, with a good balance across the disciplines and subjects within them. But class offerings in any given semester are constrained by which faculty can be recruited. Most of the professors are regular members of the Bard faculty, who are also teaching a full schedule at the Annandale campus. The rest come from neighboring institutions, such as Vassar and the State University of New York at New Paltz, or, in special cases, from more distant colleges such as Columbia, New York University, and even the Massachusetts Institute of Technology. All faculty members hold doctorates or another terminal degree. Even though they are paid a small stipend for their teaching, the draw is the intrinsic reward of teaching such engaged and hardworking students.

Another key feature of Bard's general approach that is replicated in the prisons is an emphasis on extracurricular activities. In addition to the Bard Debate Union, students are active in various clubs and associations the prison authorities allow incarcerated individuals to organize. One year, for example, an alumnus of the associate's program, who was keenly interested in history and philosophy, gave a speech to the branch of the National Association for the Advancement of Colored People organized at one of the prisons on the occasion of the 104th anniversary of the NAACP. Entitled "We Shall Endure," it built on the history of the civil rights movement to argue that current challenges to civil rights, including the recent reversal of parts of the Voting Rights Act of 1965, could best be addressed by asking every individual to "reenvision the Dream" and find personal ways to make it a reality. That same year, another student convinced his peers in the drama club to read one of the Shakespeare plays he had previously studied in a Bard class.

Once a year, Bard's president, Leon Botstein, brings the orchestra of the college's music conservatory into one of the prisons for a concert. After the performance, he takes questions, which generally range from the simple—"Why are there so many violins in the orchestra?"—to ones that reveal considerable knowledge and interest—"I wonder why you played the second movement of the Beethoven piece so fast." These concerts offer a new experience, with many students reporting that they were surprised by how much they enjoyed the music.

Whenever possible, the college program organizes lectures by visitors or faculty members. One year, I offered a four-part series on the history of American education, with each lecture covering a century of history, in the hope of triggering debate about questions such as "Is public education important in a democracy?" and "Is meritocracy a good thing?" The same year, one visitor gave a lecture about the history of sex education in American public schools, and another described the development of radical feminism. When a group of students at one of the prisons created an organic garden, a lecture series by urban farmers was offered. The garden, which applies and enriches course work in genetics and public health, provides fresh produce for the prison as well as for local homeless shelters.

Academic advisement is another important aspect of Bard's prison program, just as it is on the Annandale campus. Every student has a faculty advisor, with whom he or she meets at least three times each semester. The advisors' role is primarily to discuss academic challenges and progress to date, but sometimes they also offer advice about time management and balancing competing demands, including prison jobs, which pay needed pennies for items in the commissary; participation in mandated prison programs; physical exercise; communicating with one's family; and making time for study. Advisement within the Bard Prison Initiative goes beyond scheduled appointments. Faculty sometimes go to a prison to talk with students, sitting in the library or in study rooms to chat with whomever wants to talk. Such informal conversations with students might take the form of one-on-one discussions, but more often they involve a number of students, all of whom want to talk about some event in the news, or a book they have all read, or suggestions for improving the college program. These are prime opportunities for faculty to model effective ways to express and explain one's opinion, providing a well-reasoned rationale and welcoming thoughtful debate.

Advisement within Bard's prison program is frequent and often quite intense. It is not an add-on, undertaken by a special group of advisors whose function is really only to assist in the course selection and registration process. It is integral to the academic program and vital to the culture of aspiration that characterizes the college. Although carried on informally, advisement is not limited to faculty counseling students. It goes on among students as they share advice about everything from class papers to preparing to meet with the parole board. In fact, in discussing their Bard experience, students often state that it is the sense of comradeship with the other students as well as between students and faculty that was most important to them. Spending a lot of time with one's entering cohort fosters this. So does time spent in the study room, where informal conversations often take place. The coaching that is encouraged among students also supports the development of common bonds. When a student has special knowledge of a particular topic, he or she often becomes a resource for others. That is especially the case for bachelor's students who have completed their senior thesis and become experts on the topic they studied.

Even though Bard's incarcerated students have made their way through a rigorous liberal arts curriculum, they still need help planning for release and actually negotiating the challenges of returning to society. To provide for this, the Bard Prison Initiative offers a reentry program, which combines counseling and continuing academic work. The program begins with one-on-one meetings to help people think about the assistance they will need when they go home. Who will meet them at the prison gate? Where will they live? How can they get a New York State ID? Where can they sign up for Medicaid and public assistance? If students do not have family members who can assist with the nuts and bolts of getting on their feet, a staff member can step in. Sometimes this involves referrals to homeless shelters, halfway houses, or clinics that accept Medicaid. Sometimes it requires helping a graduate gain admission to addiction services. It might also involve discussion of how to handle issues with one's family.

Students who are released from prison before finishing their degrees are actively encouraged to continue their education. If a student is near completion, arrangements are made with a faculty advisor to help that student finish the necessary work, usually a senior thesis, and receive his or her Bard degree. If they are not so far along, they are encouraged to seek admission to another institution, most often one of the campuses of the City University of New York. The reentry program has established close relationships with several colleges and facilitates the admission of students as well as helping them obtain financial aid.

The program also helps in identifying potential employers. Bard has developed relationships with a number of companies and organizations that are willing to consider candidates with a felony conviction. Though first jobs are often low-level and may involve bagging groceries or filing in an office, as men and women demonstrate reliability, it is often possible to secure more suitable employment that will tap their interests and skills and provide a better salary.

On the academic side, the reentry program offers additional course work inside the prisons, in three areas: public health, computer science, and food systems. These are fields that connect with the knowledge and skill Bard students have developed in college, notably in math and science, and areas of employment in which alums are likely to find good jobs. A credit-bearing class is offered in each area, usually taught in collaboration with faculty from other institutions such as the Mailman School of Public Health at Columbia University, and seminars and lectures are also organized.

Although it is not officially part of the reentry program, a network of Bard Prison Initiative alums offers concrete help, advice, and social support for all Bard people returning home. Over the years spent in college classes, former students have often developed strong personal bonds, or at least common ties of loyalty to Bard, and after release these translate into a powerful willingness to help one another. In addition to providing job referrals and recommendations, former students often contact the families of their friends who remain in prison to see if they can help them out. They often include spouses in social events, or play baseball with the kids. They also remain in contact with the peers they left behind, sharing news from both sides of the prison walls. People who became friends in prison are often the first to call out a peer, and offer help, if he or she seems dangerously close to getting into any kind of trouble. They feel a common stake in ensuring that everyone does well. All graduates of the prison program are members of the Bard Alumni Association, and many attend the annual reunion as well as the one held by the prison program especially for its alums.

Contrary to the claim that "nothing works," the Bard Prison Initiative works very well. It has proven that adults who have not profited from education earlier in their lives can overcome that disadvantage and meet the challenges of an exacting, advanced education. It has demonstrated that excellence in education can be achieved inside prisons, thereby creating ladders to inclusion in American society rather than barriers to a fully engaged, productive life. Is the Bard program a model that could and should be replicated elsewhere? With assistance from Bard, almost a dozen other liberal arts colleges have launched college-in-prison programs that now operate in correctional facilities from Maryland and Connecticut in the east to Washington in the west. Along with

Bard, they are all members of the Consortium for the Liberal Arts in Prison and share Bard's insistence on academic rigor and standards set by the sponsoring college; especially if Pell eligibility is fully restored, more colleges may follow suit. Whether or not that happens, the Bard Prison Initiative is a continuing experiment in changing prisons and changing lives through expanded access to high-quality education.

8

Variety and Difference

College in Prison Across the United States

James Sellers was lucky. While he was incarcerated in Indiana, he was able to finish the course work he had started toward a bachelor's degree even after the initial college program in which he was enrolled was shut down. He had been taking classes via a program run by Ball State University, but then, in 2011, the Indiana legislature passed a law barring those in prison from receiving state grants to pay for college degrees, and Ball State and other colleges discontinued their prison college classes. Indiana had been one of only a few states that had dedicated public funds to college in prison, and according to John Nally, director of education at the Indiana Department of Correction, the state had boasted the largest participation in college programs of any state, with 10 percent of men incarcerated there taking classes and 15 percent of the women.[1] When financial aid was stopped, one thousand students in Indiana prisons were studying for Ball State degrees, which made it the largest provider of higher education in the system. James was one of the few who were able to continue their studies. He won a place in a privately funded program run jointly by Notre Dame University and Holy Cross College and finished the work needed for the bachelor's degree.

Going to college has been instrumental in helping James build a successful postprison life. His prospects would probably have been dim otherwise. He had been sentenced to fifteen years for murder, having killed a man who had been stalking his mother, and before that he had run a gang that was involved in selling drugs. He attributes his decision to commit himself to legitimate work to the new perspectives and skills he gained through his college classes. He has found a job that he enjoys, as a highly skilled aluminum cutter, assembling semitruck trailers, and he and his wife have reunited after a long separation.[2]

Most of those in prison who are eager for the chance to attend college and turn their lives around have not shared James's good fortune. Closures and cutbacks in college offerings have continued since the large-scale shutdowns that followed the 1994 elimination of Pell Grant eligibility. Although the Obama administration announced in the summer of 2015 that it would reopen Pell funding on a limited, experimental basis, recent years had seen two additional major setbacks. In 2011, the same year that Indiana passed its ban, Congress voted not to renew funding for federal grants known as Specter funds, named for the sponsoring senator, Arlen Specter. These grants had provided some financial support to the states for college classes for the incarcerated. The 2008 recession also led to significant cuts in all kinds of correctional education. A 2014 study of state correctional education systems conducted by the RAND Corporation found that the economic downturn resulted in cuts ranging from 10 to 20 percent in the larger systems, with college-level academic classes being hardest hit and a shift toward more emphasis on vocational training. One of the RAND researchers characterized the cuts as "a dramatic contraction of the prison education system, particularly those programs focused on academic instruction versus vocational training."[3]

Fortunately, even while many publicly supported programs were scaled back or closed, private funds made it possible to create others. While no comprehensive survey of current college offerings exists, a selective portrait of the major types of programs can provide a sense of today's landscape.

A broad-brush picture of college programs and students in prisons across the country can be devised from two available sources. In 2010, Kaia Stern, director of the Prison Studies Project at Harvard University's Kennedy School of Government, created an online directory of higher-education programs by state, which included forty-seven programs of various kinds. The directory is not up to date, but it offers a helpful overview. Stern found that in twenty-three states, no programs were available; in five, only non-degree-granting courses were offered; in thirteen, only one program was available; and in an additional three states—California, Georgia, and Minnesota—two programs were offered. At the high end, Oregon had four programs, Indiana had eight (now seven due to the closure of the Ball State program), and New York was home to eight.[4] The best available census of how many people are attending classes was conducted even earlier, in 2005, and reported that only 5 percent of the 1,410,404 men and women imprisoned across fifty state prison programs and in federal prisons as of 2004—or approximately 70,000—were enrolled in some form of postsecondary education.[5]

The sponsorship and focus of college-in-prison programs varies widely, mirroring the great diversity of American higher education generally. Most programs—68 percent—are branches of a community college. Others are extensions of a small liberal arts college or a large university, are administered by a specially created nonprofit organization, or are operated by state correctional systems. Some college programs offer only non-credit-bearing courses; others offer classes for college credit but do not offer degrees. Of those offering degrees, some offer only an associate's, others offer only a bachelor's, still others offer both degrees, and a few offer master's degrees. Vocational courses are the focus of some postsecondary programs, while the liberal arts are the focus of others. Some prison colleges are highly selective, while others have open enrollment, often based on the principle of first-come, first-served. Many prison systems offer access to college classes only through off-site distance-learning programs, usually of the paper-and-pencil variety, which were not included by Kaia Stern in her count.

To provide a framework for this patchwork quilt of offerings, it is useful to break them down into four basic types. Programs such as Bard's represent the first type. They are affiliated with a college, university, or nonprofit organization and, while subject to some oversight by the state correctional authorities, are not part of a correctional system. The other three types are programs run by state correctional systems, religiously affiliated programs, and ones that combine education with social activism. The types are useful for descriptive purposes, but are not absolute since some programs fit into more than one type.

Two consortia of colleges have taken the lead in expanding privately run liberal arts programs. One of these is the Consortium for the Liberal Arts in Prison, which, as mentioned earlier, has been created by the Bard Prison Initiative and is led by Bard. It includes the University of Notre Dame and Holy Cross College in Indiana, where James Sellers was enrolled; Wesleyan University in Connecticut, which has recently developed a partnership with Middlesex Community College in Connecticut; Goucher College in Maryland; Grinnell College in Iowa; the Freedom Education Project Puget Sound in Washington, which operates in collaboration with both Tacoma and Seattle Community Colleges; and Washington University in St. Louis. Two new consortium partners, Berea College in Kentucky and Minnesota State University, Mankato, are slated to begin classes in the fall of 2016. All members of the consortium adhere to the principle that men and women in prison should be offered the same challenging liberal arts experience that students enrolled at the nation's best colleges are offered. Their course work is rigorous and on a par with that of the sponsoring institution, and they are governed by faculty and administrators from the parent college. Beyond these basic standards, the programs differ in some regards.

Most of the programs have highly selective admission, with requirements akin to Bard's, and serve on the order of between twenty to thirty students at a given time, though the number varies widely. One exception to the selectivity is the program at Puget Sound, which is open to all women at the one facility where it currently operates, the Washington Corrections Center for Women. The emphasis of most of the programs is on the education of the incarcerated students, but as discussed earlier, the Grinnell program also focuses on educating main campus Grinnell students about social justice issues, with the impressive outcome that many of the participants go into community-oriented work following graduation. Several of the colleges offer bachelor's degrees, but others offer only the associate's, and some do not offer degrees at all.

The other large umbrella organization, the New York Consortium for Higher Education in Prison, is an even more varied assortment. According to Rob Scott, the executive director of the Prison Education Program at Cornell, the group was pulled together to advocate for the reestablishment of Pell Grant eligibility for people in prison. In addition to Cornell, its members are John Jay College of Criminal Justice; the Mohawk Consortium College-in-Prison Program, which involves faculty members from a number of upstate private colleges including Hamilton College and Colgate University, as well as Mohawk Valley Community College, a public institution; and Hudson Link, which is a federation joining Sienna, Nyack, Mercy, and Vassar Colleges, along with one public college, Sullivan County Community College.

In this group, one of the programs is distinctive because it is run by a publicly funded institution in conjunction with state officials. John Jay's college-in-prison program, which is known as the college's Prison-to-College Pipeline (P2CP), was launched in 2011 and operates in collaboration with the New York State Department of Corrections and Community Supervision. John Jay is part of the public City University of New York system, and a prime goal of the program is to prepare students to attend one of the City University colleges after release. The John Jay program offers academic credit-bearing course work (but no degrees), as well as remedial education. There is a strong emphasis on reentry programming, especially to help students in applying to City University for further study.

With Bard and the New York Consortium, New York State is home to the largest number of privately sponsored liberal arts college-in-prison programs. In stark contrast, California is now home to only one on-site liberal arts program, the nonprofit Prison University Project at San Quentin. This is striking, since California is one of the country's pioneers in expanding access to higher education, with its enormous state-run college and university system, and once offered state-run college programs in every one of the state's prisons. Initiated in 1994 as a protest against the elimination of Pell Grant eligibility by a group of men incarcerated at San Quentin, the Prison University Project began with two classes and now offers twenty courses during each of three semesters, approximately one-third of which are college-preparatory classes in math and English. The rest are regular college-level classes in the humanities, social sciences, math, and science. A nonprofit runs the program, rather than a college or university, with faculty members and graduate students recruited from a number of Bay Area colleges and universities to teach as volunteers. Any student who has a high school credential or who has earned a general education diploma can be admitted on a first-come, first-served basis, and there is a long waiting list. The number of students enrolled is larger than at most college programs: Administrators recently reported that 330 students were taking classes, with 400 waiting to get in. Most students take two classes a semester, each meeting for two hours twice a week, and, if they are not paroled first, complete their degrees in three and a half years.[6]

Another of the long-running privately sponsored programs has been operated by Boston University since 1972. It is the only college-in-prison program in Massachusetts that survived the elimination of Pell Grant eligibility; the other seven colleges and universities in the state that had offered bachelor's degrees, as well as several community college programs offering associate's degrees, closed their doors. Boston University operates in two facilities, the MCI/Norfolk prison for men and the MCI/Framingham prison for women, with classes taught by professors from Boston University and colleagues from neighboring institutions that do not sponsor their own programs. A large number of courses are offered across the liberal arts, leading to bachelor's degrees. Admittance is selective, with applicants required to pass a rigorous entrance exam and earn at least a 2.5 GPA in four preparatory classes in order to continue with the program.[7]

According to Kaia Stern's count in 2010, only six states in addition to New York, California, and Massachusetts are home to privately run liberal arts programs: Oregon, Kansas, Illinois, Virginia, Ohio, and New Jersey. Most of these states have only one or two college programs. Clearly, opportunities for those in prison to go to college are extremely limited nationwide, especially in comparison to the size of the incarcerated population.

State-run education programs are available to larger numbers of people, but in many states these are not college level, and for the most part the emphasis is on remedial and vocational education, with many of the higher-education classes only available through correspondence classes. Texas runs the largest state system, which is called the Windham School District. This centralized system was created in 1969 and now offers both academic and vocational education at ninety sites around the state in partnership with fourteen community colleges and three universities, as well as special education, English as a second language, and other precollege classes. The focus is remedial classes, GED preparation, and vocational training, with a wide range of trades covered, including welding, auto repair, bricklaying, hospitality and tourism, culinary arts, and computer repair. The district does offer some college classes by sending professors from seventeen two-year community colleges into 112 prisons. Students can work toward associate's and bachelor's degrees, but they can enroll for only three hours of course time per semester, and the number of academic degrees awarded in comparison to certificates for vocational training is quite small.[8] One study found that only 3 percent of students system-wide were working toward a bachelor's degree, which were available at only four of the state's prisons.[9]

New Mexico takes a dramatically different approach to making a college education available in its prisons. Its system is also centralized, and college classes can be taken at all of the state's prisons, paid for by the system, but all the courses are taught through distance learning, over a closed-circuit Internet service, with no classes taught by professors at the facilities. One four-year university, one two-year university, and a community college provide the instruction. Associate's, bachelor's, and master's degrees can be earned.[10] Enrollment in distance-learning programs offered by other institutions around the country is also allowed, but students must pay for those classes. In addition, New Mexico's prisons offer on-site vocational classes.

California is another state system that, until last year, limited access to college classes (except at San Quentin) to distance-learning offerings, but, in this case, the classes were exclusively of the older pencil-and-paper correspondence type rather than online. In a system that is home to more than 111,400 men and women, as of August 2015, only about 7,000 were enrolled in college courses leading to associate's degrees.[11] A state law passed in 2014 that allows community colleges to receive the same level of state reimbursement for courses offered in prisons as they receive for courses taken on the outside provides hope that on-site teaching will be added to the system. The law also provided for the establishment of pilot programs by four colleges, with the intention that the offerings be designed so that they could eventually be made available throughout the community college system.

The state government of North Carolina takes a third, again very different approach to centralized, state-run college programming. A 1987 law stipulated that the state's Department of Corrections work with the State Board of Community Colleges to offer a wide range of classes in the state's prisons, everything from remedial academic classes to vocational training and college offerings.[12] The state has since opened college classes to an estimated one-third of those incarcerated in its prisons, with instruction by professors from forty-nine of its fifty community colleges in eighty state prisons.[13] A notable provision of state law mandates that classes must be of the same quality as those taught on traditional campuses and no classes can be run that do not count toward a degree.[14]

North Carolina is also participating in a five-year program that is by far the most ambitious state system approach to postsecondary education in prison developed thus far. Called the Pathways from Prison to Postsecondary Education Project, it is managed by the Vera Institute of Justice and run in collaboration with three states, New Jersey and Michigan in addition to North Carolina. A group of philanthropic foundations has provided five years of funding for the initiative, with a 25 percent match of the amount received required of the participating states. Classes began in 2013. The goal is to develop and test a comprehensive, full-service model, including both vocational training and college classes, leading to degrees, along with employment and reentry counseling and parole supervision provided by specially trained parole officers.

In addition to evaluating college readiness through academic assessments of prospective students, the project works with several colleges in each state to offer classes inside prisons, which lead either to students' transfer to a local college after release or to the attainment of a degree or certificate while still incarcerated. The project is designed to build an evidence-based case about how education and postrelease programs can produce optimal outcomes, and to encourage long-term, sustainable partnerships among prisons, colleges, parole authorities, business leaders, and community agencies nationwide.

The Pathways project is up and running in two prisons in Michigan, Macomb Correctional Facility and Parnall Correctional Facility, with classes and reentry services offered by Jackson College and Kalamazoo Valley Community College. The program is more extensive in New Jersey and North Carolina. In New Jersey, three of the state's leading universities are involved, Drew University, Princeton University, and Rutgers University, as well as four community colleges, and the program provides classes in six prisons. These institutions had come together previously to form the New Jersey Scholarship and Transformative Education in Prisons Consortium, known as NJ-STEP, run in conjunction with the state's Department of Corrections. In North Carolina, six community colleges are involved at six prisons. Each of the pilot programs is somewhat different in its specifics, but they all offer tutoring and student advisement as well as substantial postrelease services, including assistance with admission to educational institutions, legal advice, and help in finding work. The RAND Corporation has been hired to conduct an evaluation of the program.[15]

Neither of the last two types of programs is purely educational in focus. The first, college programs run by religious institutions, have been growing rapidly in recent years. Saint Louis University, a Jesuit institution, which began offering a certificate program in theological studies in 2007 to men at the Eastern Reception, Diagnostic and Correctional Center in Bonne Terre, Missouri, is one example. Three years after opening, it received a grant from the Hearst Foundation, which made it possible to establish an associate's degree program for both men in custody and correctional officers. A prison program offered by Guilford College in Greensboro, North Carolina, which is a Quaker institution, is another recently initiated offering. In 2012 Guilford launched a student-designed program, which enables men held at the Piedmont Correctional Institution in Salisbury to earn Guilford degrees. The program emphasizes Quaker values and ethics as well as community service. Greenville College, a Christian college in Greenville, Illinois, is still another example of a religiously affiliated prison college. Opened in 2014, it provides credit-bearing classes in one of the federal prisons, the Federal Correctional Institution in Greenville.

A number of seminaries also offer degrees in prisons. The Southwestern Baptist Theological Seminary, whose alumni include journalist Bill Moyers and politician Mike Huckabee, recently began providing course work leading to a four-year bachelor of science degree in Biblical studies at the Darrington Unit prison in Rosharon, Texas. The first group of thirty-three students graduated in May 2015. The newly minted alums were either sent to one of six other Texas state prisons, in groups of four or five, to serve as assistant chaplains or remained at Darrington to mentor underclassmen.[16]

The Angola Seminary, created by Warden Burl Cain at the Angola prison north of New Orleans, in partnership with the New Orleans Baptist Theological Seminary, was the model for the Darrington program. When Cain arrived at Angola in 1995, he found a huge maximum-security prison, which was known for its violence. He set out to change the culture, and, as a deeply religious man, he believed that the best way to do that was through "moral rehabilitation" inspired by religious training. The New Orleans seminary now operates a fully accredited, selective, four-year college, leading to associate's or bachelor's degrees in Christian ministry, as well as a certificate program for those who cannot qualify for the degree programs. After completing their studies, the newly ordained ministers baptize, preach, and counsel their peers in the prison. The program has been effective in decreasing violence, with Angola having become one of the safest prisons in the country, but it has also been criticized for allegedly coercing men to seek religious training.[17] Critics have pointed out that the alternatives at the prison are harsh, including tough labor on the Angola farm and a disciplinary regime that relies heavily on long spells in solitary confinement. Some assert that the program violates the constitutional provision of freedom of religion.

The New York Theological Seminary, a nondenominational institution, developed the seminary program at Sing Sing correctional facility mentioned previously, which, among others, the late Eddie Ellis of the Center for NuLeadership attended, as well as some of the Bard alums. This graduate program, the only one available in a New York State prison, offers a master of professional studies degree and is highly selective, with no more than fifteen men admitted each year from a large pool of applicants. Selection is based on demonstrated promise of leadership as well as "an active faith commitment" and a willingness to move to Sing Sing, a maximum-security facility, which in many cases means transferring from a medium- or minimum-security facility. The program requires attendance at classes five days a week for a year and the successful completion of thirty-six credits. While working toward their degrees, students in this program do supervised fieldwork as peer counselors, chaplain's assistants, or tutors in one of the education programs offered at Sing Sing.[18]

The last type of college program combines education with other activities, most frequently community outreach and advocacy work, but, in an increasing number of cases, entrepreneurship training. Educational institutions run some of these programs, while others are operated by nonprofit organizations. The Education Justice

Project, which is part of the University of Illinois at Urbana-Champaign, is one example. Since 2008, it has offered upper-division credit-bearing courses taught by university faculty and graduate students at the Danville Correctional Center. It also supports a wide range of extracurricular activities at Danville, including a theater initiative, reading groups, guest lectures, and math, science, computer, and writing workshops. The program includes outreach to the families of its incarcerated students and to those who have been released via support group meetings. One recent outreach initiative, called "The Ripple Effect," officially dubbed Reaching Inside Prisons with Purpose and Love, invited members of the community to come together for a meal the third Monday of every month and to write letters and cards to people in prison. As a form of advocacy, the program sponsors annual conferences on college in prison and seeks to foster scholarship about criminal justice policies and politics in other ways as well.[19]

The Inside-Out Prison Exchange Program, based at Temple University in Philadelphia, is another example of mixed education and advocacy. It facilitates partnerships between institutions of higher education and correctional systems around the country. The core of the program consists of semester-long prison-based seminars led by faculty from the partner colleges that bring together roughly fifteen undergraduates from a college's main campus and fifteen incarcerated students. The seminars carry credit toward degrees for students from the partner colleges, but the incarcerated students are not on tracks that lead to degrees. The Inside-Out Center describes the mission as seeking to "deepen the conversation about and transform our approaches to understanding crime, justice, freedom, inequality, and other issues of social concern."[20] Begun in 1997, with a course offered by Temple faculty entitled "Exploring Issues of Crime and Justice Behind the Walls," the program has now offered more than three hundred classes. Most seminars deal with traditional college subject matter, but they are expressly designed both to inform students from the partner college about life inside prisons and to encourage incarcerated students to discuss their crimes. The hope is that by studying together and engaging in collaborative final projects, individuals in the two groups will be able to shed stereotypes and form lasting partnerships in support of education in prison and criminal justice reform.

Hybrid programs combining academic and vocational study with a focus on entrepreneurship come in a variety of formats. The Prison Entrepreneurship Program in Texas, mentioned earlier, is a prominent example. Recall that the program recruits men from many different Texas prisons and moves them to the Cleveland Correctional Facility, where they engage in classes designed to build character alongside business training activities. To help graduates with reentry, the program runs two transitional homes, in Houston and Dallas, where they can live for several months after release, and they are also provided with clothing suitable for business interviews and meetings.[21] A study conducted by faculty from Baylor University's Institute for Studies of Religion found that since 2010, all of the participants who stayed with the program to completion found a job within ninety days of release, and, though the study did not indicate what those jobs were or how many involved newly created entrepreneurial ventures, a staff member indicated that many were in lines of work with relatively few barriers for former felons, such as truck driving.[22] In 2013, the business school at Baylor established a partnership with this program, which provides for the awarding of certificates in entrepreneurship.

There are now many other entrepreneurship programs, both inside prisons and on the outside. One, called Hustling Legit, is open to those incarcerated at the Bedford Hills facility for women as well as at the Greene Correctional Facility for men in upstate New York. The Nurturing a New Start program, offered at the Kent County Correctional Facility near Grand Rapids, Michigan, and at the Community Reentry Center, which is a nearby work-release program, includes classes in financial literacy and basic business skills, as well as mentoring by both former students and business-people from the surrounding communities.

Each type of postsecondary education currently offered in the prisons has its advocates and all have pros and cons, but few, if any, have been thoroughly described and assessed. The lack of comprehensive data about the range of offerings and their relative effectiveness is unfortunate because it both impedes improvement and makes advocacy less persuasive than it might be with more evidence. Some college and university leaders have worried that college-in-prison programs would not be able to maintain their institution's high standards, thereby damaging a college's reputation. More and better evidence of positive outcomes as well as more precise information about costs and benefits might help counter such concerns. Being able to explain which practices are most likely to advance which goals, whether those are reducing recidivism or encouraging responsible citizenship, or, on another side of the equation, offering a richer understanding of social justice issues to main campus students, would also help advocates make the case to college authorities and even the public at large. More comprehensive assessments of the relative merits of different approaches would also likely be instrumental in assuring public officials not only that public funding is warranted, but that it is being marshaled in the most efficient and effective ways possible. The 2013 study by the RAND Corporation evaluating the findings from the best existing studies was a significant step forward. But more credible, outside research is needed to delve into the merits of different designs.

The pluses and minuses of having so many prison colleges linked to community colleges rather than four-year institutions is one of the most important issues in need of study. As was indicated earlier, fully 68 percent of college-in-prison programs are branches of a community college. On the positive side, community college classes are considerably less expensive than those offered by most four-year institutions. On average, tuition and fees at community colleges are $2,272 annually, in comparison to $5,836 at public four-year colleges.[23] Lower costs are important both to state authorities, in those states that provide some funding for college in prison, and to students, who sometimes must pay for some or all of their tuition, as well as for other fees, books, and supplies. Often they must do so out of their own funds, or with family support, though some states offer funding through plans that require repayment postrelease.

While the lower cost of community college is a significant plus, the low completion rates for students in community college programs, both those on the outside and in prisons, present a troubling minus. This is the case across the nation, with completion rates often running below 20 percent and sometimes in the single digits.[24] This is due to many different factors, including the remedial character of many community college classes, which are generally not as engaging to students as higher-level college classes, and too much random course taking, which is expensive and often does not lead to degrees. Moving to a different correctional facility before completion, usually because of rules pertaining to eligibility for a lower level of security, is another important factor for incarcerated students who do not complete degrees, whether enrolled in a community college or a four-year degree program. Such moves can mean that a student lands in a prison where his or her college does not operate and no other college is available. The causes for low completion rates, where they exist, warrant further study, especially in light of the finding of the RAND study that earning a degree or a certificate offers distinct advantages over just taking some classes. Completion with a degree or certificate in hand promotes success in finding work after release and not returning to prison.

Another major limitation of community college–run programs is that the curricula generally offered in prisons are heavily vocational in focus, usually providing quite specific occupational training for jobs in such fields as air-conditioning and refrigeration, data processing, graphic arts, welding, or masonry. Men and women in prison are often eager for vocational training, believing it will provide them the best chance of securing postrelease employment. Given that the history of prison education programs underscores the importance of allowing for choice and the freedom to pursue personal interests, offering opportunities to pursue vocational training is a plus. However, in our rapidly shifting economy, people should expect to work in several different jobs through the course of their work lives, and specific vocational training does not prepare people well for making those changes. Ideally, a higher-level liberal arts program should also be available because, as discussed earlier, such programs build the fundamental learning, critical thinking, and communications skills that are so important to success in work today, and will be in such demand in coming years.

Additional questions concerning the quality of the postsecondary education offered in prisons include whether all faculty should hold terminal degrees, usually a doctorate, and whether courses taught by graduate students or undergraduates, or even by a facility's correctional education staff, show outcomes different from those taught by instructors holding a doctorate. Assessments should gauge the effectiveness of different strategies for distance learning. While there is evidence that traditional correspondence-style classes are inferior to in-person instruction, much innovation is under way in computer-based distance teaching, and the learning that can be derived from various online approaches should be carefully considered in relation to whether or not such offerings should be expanded.

The appropriate emphasis on the education of incarcerated students versus that of main campus students who participate in some college-in-prison programs is another key issue that should be investigated. Bard and many other colleges give priority in their prison programs to the education of the incarcerated students, while other prison colleges, notably the one run by Grinnell, place more emphasis on enriching the educational experience of main campus students and encouraging them to become more service oriented. Do the two approaches result in differences in student experience, both on the main campuses and in the prisons, or in different outcomes? One study has made a start at discerning whether there are significant differences. Jeffrey Jurgens, a Bard faculty member, conducted a survey in 2013–14 of main campus students involved in four of the college-in-prison programs in the Consortium for the Liberal Arts in Prison (Bard, Grinnell, Wesleyan, and Goucher). He found that students' participation had a comparable effect on them across the prison programs whether emphasis was placed on educating main campus students or not. Of the 195 students who completed questionnaires, 87 percent "agreed" or "strongly agreed" that the experience had "changed their beliefs and attitudes about education and incarceration"; 74 percent said the experience had a "positive" or "extremely positive" effect on their academic work generally; and 61 percent reported that the experience had shaped their postgraduation plans.[25] Simply by offering volunteer opportunities, amounting in some cases to little more than doing library research for incarcerated students, college-in-prison programs appear to exercise a powerful formative influence on undergraduates at the sponsoring institution. Clearly, however, more extensive investigations are needed in order to come to a firm conclusion about this.

How effectively programs can be scaled up while also maintaining high quality is another significant question. Can educational institutions and departments of correction, as well as state government agencies and other service providers, notably nonprofits, coordinate well in providing comprehensive and effective college programs? Offering a model for this is part of the mission of the Pathways project, and though a full evaluation of its success in establishing good coordination is yet to come, the experience to date indicates that this will be a significant challenge. According to Fred Patrick, director of the Vera Institute's Center on Sentencing and Corrections, who oversees the project, an evaluation of the project's initial model conducted by the RAND Corporation noted that difficulties have arisen due to profound differences in the cultures of the different groups involved.[26]

One thorny problem has been concerns of correctional officials about security. For example, in both Michigan and North Carolina, participation in the project is restricted to low-level offenders and requires "behavioral contracts." Such conditions may well diminish the sense of freedom students feel as a result of participating in college programs, which the history of education in prison has shown is instrumental to educational success. Allowing security considerations to play a part in college programs may also undermine confidence among incarcerated students that they are being treated as true college students, which interviews with many students have indicated was so important to their appreciation of and commitment to their college work. Conclusions about this matter must await the full evaluation RAND will carry out at the end of the Pathways project's first five years. But the project represents a step toward the kind of experimentation and evaluation that the field of college in prison needs.

If and when more institutions step into the college-in-prison arena, other questions about the relative merits of different approaches will doubtless emerge. Pursuing those questions will help ensure that college-in-prison programs offer their students the high-quality instruction they want and deserve. That is especially important in prison settings, where students cannot "shop around" or voice dissatisfaction as students on the outside can. Research carried out as an integral part of college opportunities should serve as a much-needed safeguard, helping to guarantee that what is presented as a college experience truly meets reasonable criteria for high-quality teaching and learning at an advanced level. That said, it is worth emphasizing that calling for more research should not in any way obscure what is known already. Even though it has been well established that, across all types, college-in-prison programs provide a wide range of benefits, they remain in short supply. That must change and access to financial aid must be restored. With growing interest in "college for all" as well as widespread interest in reducing the prison population, those are realistic goals.

Conclusion

College for All

Antoine Patton is a Bard alumnus living in Florida and working as a software programmer. He has also created a nonprofit organization named the Photo Patch Foundation to receive contributions to cover the costs of enabling children to send letters and photographs to their incarcerated parents. When asked how he had figured out how to create a nonprofit organization in his first few months home from prison, he shrugged and said, "I read about it and talked to a lot of people." Like other young entrepreneurs, he embodies the initiative, imagination, and civic-mindedness that are needed to counter the many problems this country faces. He also demonstrates some of the returns that can be expected from making college accessible to people in prison. Antoine has a daughter and knows firsthand the pain of parent-child separation, and his college experience endowed him not only with the determination to do something to lessen that pain, but also with the capacity to ask questions, do research, and figure things out on his own.[1]

Antoine may be a particularly impressive go-getter, but going to college in prison almost always enhances the chances that formerly incarcerated men and women will be successful when they return to their communities. Overwhelming evidence, from both research studies and individuals' life stories, attests that college-in-prison programs offer significant benefits, not only for the people who enroll, but for their families and neighbors, and for all of us. The challenge today is building on this evidence to win public backing for providing the financial assistance those in prison need to pay for college.

Growing support for "college for all" among business leaders and policy makers makes that a realistic goal. The arguments for expanding opportunity generally also apply to extending opportunity to the incarcerated.

The most basic arguments are economic. Research has shown that the country needs many more college graduates in order to meet the future demands of the labor market and stay competitive globally. One key factor holding the number of graduates down is the escalating cost of college, which has excluded some potential students and has saddled many graduates with exorbitant student loan debt. While cutting the cost of college must be a goal, the best way to ensure that enough people get the education they need is to offer public support to the largest possible pool of potential applicants, including those in prison who want to go to college and are qualified to do so. Those who get a good education while in prison can then contribute to meeting this vital national challenge.

To understand the need for public action, it is useful to look back to 1965, when the federal government first began to guarantee student loans, and to survey how substantially costs have risen. Since that time, it has become common to borrow money to pay for college tuition and associated college fees for everything from laboratory usage to athletic equipment. Borrowing has also increased because the salary hike that comes from earning a college degree has increased, with only occasional dips over the years. That has made college more attractive and boosted enrollments. In the face of solid student demand, colleges have passed on to students the rising costs they, too, have shouldered, for everything from technology, library materials, and an expanded array of student services, to health benefits for personnel and energy costs. Between 2000 and 2013, the cost of going to college increased more than costs for health care, housing, and all other items included in the Consumer Price Index. By 2007, almost half of all college students had a federally guaranteed loan. By 2012, median student loan debt was $26,600. Among the more than 2 million students enrolled in for-profit institutions, such as Kaplan University and the University of Phoenix, which are more expensive than nonprofit and public colleges, the average debt per borrower was $32,700.[2]

With costs and debt rising, it is perhaps not surprising that graduation rates have not risen to meet the nation's need for more college graduates. But the trend is still worrying. Whereas for decades the United States led the world in college completion rates, and still did as recently as 1990, slippage in the twenty-first century has resulted in the United States dropping by 2014 to nineteenth among the twenty-eight nations studied by the Organisation for Economic Co-operation and Development. "Educational mobility" has also decreased, with fewer young people gaining more education than their parents. This slide in educational attainment has serious implications for the country's overall economic health, for individuals' earning potential, and also for community engagement and trust in government.[3]

The country is already failing to produce enough college-educated workers to meet labor market demand, and research indicates the shortfall will worsen over time. According to the Georgetown University Center on Education and the Workforce, by 2018 roughly 60 percent of all jobs will require at least some postsecondary education. To fill these positions, the United States will have to produce 22 million new college graduates with at least an associate's degree. That is some 3 million more graduates than are currently receiving degrees.[4] Recent evidence from California points in the same direction. By 2025, 41 percent of all jobs in that state will require a bachelor's degree, but only 35 percent of working-age adults will hold that credential.[5] The Pathways to Prosperity Project at the Harvard Graduate School of Education has echoed the claim that the United States is not producing enough college graduates, while also noting that "middle-skilled" workers are particularly in demand. These are people who hold associate's degrees or occupational certificates that enable them to fill jobs as electricians, construction managers, dental hygienists, paralegals, and police officers.[6]

In their 2008 book, *The Race Between Education and Technology,* Harvard economists Claudia Goldin and Lawrence F. Katz present a historical case for the importance of the country investing in education to stimulate productivity and economic growth. During the first seventy years of the twentieth century, the United States invested heavily in public schooling, more so than any other nation, making first high schools and then colleges widely available to both men and women. This unusual level of investment resulted in increased productivity, greater aggregate growth, a higher standard of living, and less inequality.

But things stalled beginning in the 1970s, when gains in productivity and wage growth slowed, inequality increased, and advances in education reached a plateau. To recapture the momentum of the earlier era, Goldin and Katz look to education, the engine of earlier advances. They also point out that investments in increased college access and degree attainment will benefit everyone because economic growth has many positive corollary outcomes, including better health and declines in crime. They urge policies to provide "quality" preschool for all children, improved K–12 schooling with more young people graduating from high school ready for college, and financial aid for college that is "sufficiently generous and transparent" so that all prepared students can earn a four-year degree or marketable skills at a community college.[7] Their argument has been widely praised and it reinforces the logic of the college-for-all movement, including the importance of including the incarcerated in the expansion of opportunity.

President Obama joined the growing ranks of supporters of college for all in 2010, and later added an endorsement of college in prison by establishing a pilot program to test the results of reinstating Pell Grant eligibility for the incarcerated. In a speech at the University of Texas at Austin he announced that raising graduation rates and making college affordable for all was "the economic issue of our time."[8] Then, in his 2015 State of the Union address, he offered a plan to address the issue, announcing that he wanted to make "two years of college . . . as free and universal in America as high school is today."[9] Soon thereafter, two Democrats, Senator Tammy Baldwin of Wisconsin and Representative Bobby Scott of Virginia, introduced a bill called the America's College Promise Act of 2015, which would provide $79.7 billion over ten years to enable states to provide first-time students with full-tuition waivers to enroll in two-year programs. The bill stipulated that those programs must either have agreements providing for student transfer to four-year public institutions or certificate programs in occupations with known high demand. As then secretary of education Arne Duncan explained in a speech at the University of Maryland, Baltimore County, if passed, this bill would make "two years of college as universal as high school became in the 20th century to the great benefit of our nation's economy."[10] The Commission on Inclusive Prosperity, co-chaired by former secretary of the Treasury Lawrence H. Summers and a British counterpart, former member of Parliament Ed Balls, also favored such action, arguing that the United States "should make higher education virtually free at a community college or a public four-year college so that all high school graduates and their families have no doubt that they can afford higher education."[11]

Unfortunately, despite strong public support for making college more affordable, with polls showing that almost all Americans are in favor of expanding access to higher education, the bill met with opposition. Republican leaders immediately labeled the plan "incomplete, ill-targeted, and dead-on-arrival."[12] Senator Lamar Alexander, the Tennessee Republican who chairs the Senate Health, Education, Labor, and Pensions committee, took the lead in criticizing the bill, insisting that new plans to support college access should be generated by the states rather than the federal government. The America's Promise Act has therefore not made headway in Congress, although there are promising signs of progress on other fronts.

It is certainly a good omen that each of the Democratic presidential candidates and one of the Republican candidates (Jeb Bush) who ran in the 2015 presidential primaries touted a college-for-all plan. The proposals differed significantly with Bernie Sanders favoring no tuition, Hillary Clinton wanting generous scholarships and lower interest on loans, and Jeb Bush urging that the federal government provide up to $50,000 per student as a line of credit to be repaid during the first twenty-five years after graduation. Despite these differences, all three candidates favored college for all in the sense that they wanted the financial barriers to college attendance removed so that college is accessible to all who meet the academic requirements.

Another hopeful sign for college for all is the effort to translate public opinion into advocacy at the state and local levels that is being led by a group of businesspeople, politicians, and educators in Washington State, who banded together in 2014 to launch the Campaign for Free College Tuition. A centerpiece is a proposal for National Promise Scholarships. These would provide two years of community college tuition for all graduating high school students whose families had annual incomes under $180,000. In addition, four years of tuition at public or private colleges would be available for those with high grades and acceptances from four-year institutions. The campaign has thrown the spotlight on the seventy-five "promise scholarship" programs that already operate across the country, the first of which was launched in 2005 in Kalamazoo, Michigan. Two states, Tennessee and Oregon, have announced they will offer scholarships by the fall of 2016. Many counties and cities have also announced plans to do so.[13]

Tennessee, where a college-for-all plan is already in operation, developed the first statewide plan. Any senior who graduates from high school is eligible to apply for the Tennessee Promise, which provides "last dollar" scholarships to supplement other aid, particularly Pell Grants, for students enrolling in any of Tennessee's twenty-seven technical colleges, thirteen community colleges, or other in-state four-year public universities offering an associate's degree. The program covers only certificates and two-year degrees because that is where labor market demand is forecast to be greatest. In addition, two-year colleges are seen as cost-effective and offer remedial classes, which 70 percent of high school graduates are expected to need. All students who apply to the Tennessee Promise are also assigned a volunteer mentor, who will serve as "an encourager and task master." The program has limits. For example, older adults returning to school are not eligible for funds, nor are non–U.S. citizens. But it is designed to ensure access and attainment for all traditional-age American students.[14]

Beginning in the fall of 2015, the city of Chicago also implemented a college scholarship plan. All graduates of the Chicago Public Schools who maintain a 3.0 grade-point average and pass completion tests in math and English are encouraged to apply for Star Scholarships to help pay for three years of college, the assumption being that it will take them three years to complete a two-year degree. The scholarships cover that part of tuition, fees, and books not covered by other federal or state funding. They can be used at any one of the City Colleges of Chicago, the two-year community colleges that have developed career pathways to prepare people for jobs in growing industries as well as transfer relationships with four-year institutions. The plan also includes a dual-enrollment arrangement, which allows up to four thousand public school students to begin college classes free of charge while completing their junior or senior years of high school.[15]

As momentum has built for such financial support, the argument that incarcerated individuals should be included in college-for-all plans has also gained traction, most notably with President Obama's Pell Grant announcement. In July of 2015, the administration unveiled what it called the Second Chance Pell Pilot program. This will enable people now in prison, especially those who are five years or less away from going home, to enroll in "high quality" postsecondary education and training. Describing the plan, then secretary of education Arne Duncan said, "America is a nation of second chances. Giving people who have made mistakes in their lives a chance to get back on track and become contributing members of society is fundamental to who we are—it can also be a cost-saver for taxpayers." The Pell pilot, he continued, will help to fulfill the "Obama Administration's commitment to create a fairer, more effective criminal justice system, reduce recidivism, and combat the impact of mass incarceration on communities." The pilot also fulfills the Department of Education's mandate under the Higher Education Act "to periodically administer experiments to test the effectiveness of statutory and regulatory flexibility for participating postsecondary institutions in disbursing federal student aid."[16]

Educators and politicians as well as the editorial pages of newspapers around the country have applauded the Pell pilot announcement. New Jersey's *Star-Ledger* announced that "giving an inmate a shot at college is completely in line with . . . the small government desire to reform a big expensive prison system that isn't working."[17] *USA Today* published a piece by Loretta Lynch and Arne Duncan on its editorial page, noting: "The Obama administration has taken an important step toward helping people in prison contribute to the economy, transition back into their communities and stay out of the justice system after they reenter society. . . . And that is fundamentally good for America."[18] Claiming that the 1994 decision to remove Pell eligibility from people living behind bars had been a "dumb move," the *New York Times* simply said, "College prison programs have more than proved their worth."[19]

At the same time, establishing the Pell pilot program reignited the political opposition that has blocked previous efforts to restore financial aid for people in prison. Even though being tough on crime is no longer the litmus test for politicians it had become when the 1994 crime bill was passed, granting the incarcerated rights to postsecondary education is still controversial in some quarters. When Senator Lamar Alexander heard of the initiative, he berated the Obama administration for "making yet another end run around Congress." Even as he acknowledged that giving Pell Grants to some prisoners might be "a worthwhile idea," he claimed that matters concerning the balance of power between the federal government and the states were even more important, insisting that "the administration absolutely does not have the authority to do this."[20] Then, Representative Chris Collins, a New York State Republican, introduced legislation to block the Pell pilot program, stating that it would inappropriately "put the cost of a free college education for criminals on the backs of the taxpayers."[21] He further asserted that making grants available to the incarcerated would mean that "the Pell Grant is not going to a middle-class family struggling to pay tuition." As a National Public Radio report pointed out, he was wrong; Pell Grants go to anyone who meets the grant's financial criteria, so opening them to people in prison would not involve taking them away from other people.[22]

To anyone who has followed the issue, the objections Collins raised are familiar. In New York, Governor Andrew Cuomo's February 2014 proposal to provide financial aid for college to people in prison was quickly withdrawn as a result of opposition just like that Collins expressed. At the time, State Senator Greg Ball, who had begun a petition drive labeled "Hell No to Attica University," had asserted that college financial aid for prisoners was "a slap in the face to hard working New Yorkers that work multiple jobs and take out exorbitant student loans to pay for the cost of college." Echoing the refrain, Mark Grisanti, a Republican state senator from Buffalo, argued in favor of increased financial assistance for "hard-working, law-abiding citizens" rather than for criminals.[23] Foreshadowing the subsequent dissent from the Obama plan, the New York fight was premised on the objection raised by Jesse Helms, the late Republican senator from North Carolina, in 1991: that it is unfair to offer prisoners assistance when "hardworking, law-abiding" citizens have so much trouble paying for college.

For a variety of procedural reasons, Helms's proposal was defeated that year. But when it was reintroduced in 1993, as an amendment to the crime bill that became law in 1994, the fairness argument held sway. First-term senator Kay Bailey Hutchison, a Republican from Texas, proposed the exclusion of prisoners from Pell Grants on the grounds that "the American people are frustrated by a federal government and a Congress that cannot seem to get priorities straight. They are frustrated and angered by a federal government that sets rules that put convicts at the head of the line for college financial aid, crowding out law-abiding citizens."[24] The amendment passed by a large majority.

The reason the fairness argument has been compelling to some people is clear: college *is* expensive, and hardworking, law-abiding people *do* struggle to pay college bills. The logic of the argument is not sound, however. Simple eligibility for Pell Grants did not and would not, as Hutchison asserted, put people in prison at the head of the line for funds, and it would not take grants away from other students. The argument also entirely disregards the economic benefits to the country. Not only does the nation need more people to receive higher education, but the studies cited earlier about reduced recidivism indicate that including the incarcerated in college-for-all plans will cost less than continuing to pay for cycles of incarceration and may well also lead to net economic gains.

Reopening access to postsecondary education for men and women in prison is also in keeping with the historic trajectory of education in the United States. As Claudia Goldin and Lawrence F. Katz demonstrated, the country has consistently offered higher levels of education to more people, and reaped great benefits from doing so. At the college and university level, expanding access has often involved public funding, first in the form of land grants to support the establishment and operation of colleges and universities, notably the agricultural and mechanics colleges founded through the Civil War–era Morrill Act. Later, grants and loans to cover the enrollment costs for individual students were made available, initially to returning GIs, then to people pursuing degrees in fields deemed to be of strategic national need in fighting the Cold War, and finally to people with demonstrated financial need. Those in Congress who argue that the federal government should not be proposing expanded funding, or offering it to people in prison, are disavowing the vital role this tradition of publicly supported access has played in strengthening our economy and democracy.

Fortunately, even as politicians debate President Obama's Pell Pilot program, efforts are under way to demonstrate both the feasibility of expanding college-in-prison offerings and the value of doing so. The most complete recent plan for such colleges was developed by a public-private partnership called the Renewing Communities Initiative. Officials from the California state government collaborated with representatives from a consortium of private foundations to commission an extensive study of college-in-prison programs around the country. Carried out by a team of researchers from UC Berkeley and Stanford, the study involved organizing a two-day meeting of roughly 150 experts in corrections and higher education, conducting an in-depth examination of relevant research literature and government reports, and interviewing some 175 individuals, including both students in college-in-prison programs and education and corrections administrators. The report that resulted, which was issued in 2015 and entitled *Degrees of Freedom*, proposed a statewide plan for colleges in prisons that was intended to establish guidelines for similar programs across the nation. Some of the details about funding and possible partner programs are California-specific and will not pertain to other states, but the general model has wide relevance.

The plan builds on the three-tiered college system pioneered in California, following recommendations advanced in the 1960 California Master Plan for Higher Education. This encompasses community colleges, open to all applicants over eighteen years of age, high school degree or not; state universities, which admit the top third of graduating high school students; and the nine University of California campuses, which are research institutions offering undergraduate, graduate, and professional degrees on a competitive entry basis. The *Degrees of Freedom* report recommends that the California system be expanded to include partnerships with jails and prisons to offer a comparable range of opportunity. Corrections officials would work with neighboring community college personnel, as well as with more distant state and university leaders, to provide postsecondary instruction both inside jails and prisons and on the outside. Recognizing that formerly incarcerated individuals are likely to need help with housing and employment, the report additionally calls for the involvement of a wide range of community agencies to assist with postrelease success. The Renewing Communities Initiative is now involved in the creation of a number of initial college-in-prison programs across the state according to the report's recommendations.

The Stanford and Berkeley scholars who wrote the *Degrees of Freedom* report outline a number of design principles that are essential to the success of programs, assuring that the opportunities colleges offer are high quality and are fully embraced by students.

The first of these is that education programs must conceive of participants as students rather than prisoners and address them that way. Highlighting the essential differences between the ways institutions of education and criminal justice systems view the individuals who pass through them, the authors observe, "Colleges and universities teach students by exposing them to new ideas and skills, instilling a thirst for inquiry and cultivating leadership; correctional institutions confine inmates and prioritize the safety and security of their facilities by enforcing compliance and restricting individuality."[25] Insisting that students be seen and treated as students may seem insignificant, but it can shape the way faculty members interact with students as well as how students feel about themselves while they are engaged in classes. The report emphasizes that treating an incarcerated person as a free man or woman can be transformative for them, offering opportunities for self-assertion and self-definition that build confidence, discipline, and ambition.

The Bard Prison Initiative, among others, shares this conviction and has shown how powerful the effect can be. No security personnel are posted in the Bard study rooms or classes, and disciplinary infractions do not disqualify students. The particular design of the Bard program, replicating as it does the full Bard curriculum, is by no means the only way to offer students a high-quality collegiate experience—excellence comes in many forms. What matters, and matters vitally, is that colleges in prison must be colleges, first and foremost, and not part of a correctional regime. To the extent possible, the fact that they operate behind bars must be irrelevant. Finding ways to create free spaces for education within institutions designed to constrain freedom is difficult, but it can and must be done.

The second design principle advocated in the *Degrees of Freedom* report is that the curriculum, standards, and academic policies of college-in-prison programs must be identical to those in place at the home campus and set by educators rather than security personnel. The faculty teaching inside correctional facilities must hold the same credentials as those teaching at the home campus, and they must be held to the same expectations for class preparation and student feedback. Grading policies must also be the same. The goal of college-in-prison programs must be to include the incarcerated in the state's overall efforts to increase its college-educated workforce and citizenry, and not to offer an inferior, second-class experience.

The report additionally advises that every college-in-prison program, along with any programs for the formerly incarcerated offered in their home communities, have a dedicated program coordinator to help students find necessary services and to ensure that the academic resources and faculty available to them are of high quality. This recommendation wisely acknowledges that, as is the case with so many nonincarcerated students who enroll in community colleges, the weak educational preparation of most students needs to be acknowledged and addressed. Too often, education institutions have already failed these students; too often, these students have flunked out or been pushed out of school before graduating. Many therefore lack study skills; others are missing basic academic skills in language and mathematics. Some may require tutoring or placement in a study group. Careful and sometimes intense advisement is essential so students are counseled to enroll in courses that lead to degrees and careers. Random course taking does not add up to academic success. Counselors are also expected to refer students to appropriate community services to assist with housing, health, or financial needs. This will help ensure that nonacademic problems do not interfere with persistence toward earning a degree.

An important provision of the *Degrees of Freedom* report is that there be ongoing, rigorous evaluation of the college programs that are created. This is vital because it will determine whether the caliber of the faculty, the focus of the classes, and the excellence of the instruction are on par with the report's recommendations, and it will help to establish whether high-quality programs can be offered in prisons at a large scale. If the principles enunciated in the report are translated into practice, California's long tradition of leadership in providing equal access to high-quality postsecondary education will be greatly enhanced, and other states will have a strong model to draw on in designing their own college-in-prison programs.

Quality controls will be crucial if and when more college programs are created. Arne Duncan underscored this mandate when he announced the Second Chance Pell Pilot program, indicating that only "high quality" programs would be included in the initiative. Defining "high quality" has always been difficult in higher education, with views differing on matters such as the value of liberal arts versus vocational education and the merits of different modes of instruction. This last issue is becoming more heated as technology offers new opportunities to provide instruction cheaply and on a large scale. While problems of quality have been documented across types of institutions, special note must be made of criticisms of for-profit colleges. If Pell Grant eligibility is reinstated for the incarcerated, for-profit institutions are likely to be avid providers of college-in-prison programs, and close regulation and scrutiny of them will be required. These institutions have business plans mandating continuously growing enrollment, but often lack incentives to ensure completion of degrees or that students are learning. They are also relatively expensive, and students enrolled in them have accumulated more student loan debt than those going to nonprofit schools. They also have higher default rates. In addition, 72 percent of the people who have gone through their employment programs make less money than high school dropouts.[26]

As a result of these issues, the Obama administration has imposed strict regulations on profit-making colleges and universities, designed to increase completion rates, ensure that certificate programs match up with licensure requirements, and restrain charges to students.[27] Those regulations will have to be intensely enforced and the prison programs continuously monitored to ensure that students get the "high quality" education that the Pell program is intended to diffuse.

There are many challenges involved in offering people in prison access to first-rate higher education, but we live at a moment in time when the chances of meeting those challenges are high. The wide and strong support for college for all should provide the momentum. In the last few years, there has been a sea change in public opinion about mass incarceration. As Marc Mauer and David Cole point out in an op-ed piece in the *New York Times*, when Hillary Rodham Clinton, Ted Cruz, Eric H. Holder Jr., Jeb Bush, George Soros, Marco Rubio, and Charles G. Koch are all lined up to bring mass imprisonment to an end, it is safe to say the tide has turned.[28] Linking advocacy for college in prison to calls for college for all can propel a similar change of view about offering the incarcerated access to college. Road maps such as that provided by the *Degrees of Freedom* report can additionally offer guidance as to how high standards can be achieved at reasonable cost.

If it is time to cut the numbers of people we incarcerate, as it surely is, and to shorten unduly long sentences, it is also time to offer people in prison opportunities to realize their potential. It is time to make access to college in prison a reality for all who want it.

Acknowledgments

This book has evolved a lot since its inception and it has taken a long time to complete. Many friends, colleagues, and new acquaintances have provided information or read and commented on drafts. Rather than list them all here, I will look forward to thanking them in person. I am very grateful for their wisdom and help.

When I was first thinking about this book, Dashiell Farewell and, later, Jessica Lipschultz helped dig up material in various libraries. Susan Heath read an early draft and taught me a lot over not-very-good lunches in Pete's Famous Restaurant in Rhinebeck, New York. While I was working on the final draft, Emily Loose helped find additional sources and offered editorial suggestions on the entire manuscript. The book is better for her work. Diane Wachtell took time from a packed schedule to read and comment on successive drafts, in the process skillfully streamlining the book's logic and organization. The staff at The New Press did a superb job of copyediting and producing the book. Thanks to you all.

The staff and faculty of the Bard Prison Initiative are an extraordinary group of very hardworking and dedicated people. Their willingness to share their knowledge and insight and to provide information when I needed it went far beyond the call of duty. Their constant good humor as we have waited to go into prisons, walked the long hallways, haggled over entrance exams, and debated ways to help students through difficult classes and senior projects has always astounded me. They have been colleagues par excellence.

I owe a special debt to Max Kenner and Daniel Karpowitz, who together built the Bard Prison Initiative, taking it from its modest, if ambitious, beginnings to the large and successful college program it is today. Max was the person who convinced me to try teaching in a prison; Daniel was the person who escorted me into the Eastern Correctional Facility for my first class. I am tremendously grateful to both of them for inviting me to join them in all aspects of this challenging, satisfying, and fun work.

As always, my family has made me laugh, play, and put my writing aside. My husband Kord is, among many other things, the most patient person and best listener I know. This book would not have seen the light of day without him.

The book is dedicated to the Bard Prison Initiative's students, who have taught me a great deal about teaching, learning, perseverance, courage, and humor, not to mention the realities of American society. May you always flourish and be proud of your accomplishments.

Notes

Introduction

1. This is a paraphrase from memory, and not a direct quote.

2. Bruce Western, *Punishment and Inequality in America* (New York: Russell Sage, 2006), 111.

3. "About Hudson Link for Higher Education in Prison," http://www.hudsonlink.org/about/why-prison-education.

4. "Overview: Cornell University Prison Education Program," http://cpep.cornell.edu.

5. Eric Westervelt, "Why Aren't There More Higher Education Programs Behind Bars," 7 September 2015, *All Things Considered*, National Public Radio, http://www.npr.org/sections/ed/2015/09/07/436342257/prison-university-project.

6. Lawrence H. Summers and Ed Balls, "Report of the Commission on Inclusive Prosperity" (Washington, D.C.: Center for American Progress, 2015), 136, https://cdn.americanprogress.org/wp-content/uploads/20015/01/1PC-PDV-full.pdf.

7. "State Spending for Corrections: Long-Term Trends and Recent Criminal Justice Policy Reforms," 11 September 2013, https://www.nasbo.org/sites/default/files/pdf/State%20Spending%20for%20Corrections.pdf.

8. NAACP Smart and Safe Campaign, "Misplaced Priorities: Over Incarcerate, Under Educate," 2nd ed. (May 2011), 7, 13.

9. "State of Recidivism: The Revolving Door of America's Prisons," Pew Charitable Trusts, 2011, http://www.pewtrusts.org/en/about/news-room

/press-releases/0001/01/01/pew-finds-four-in-10-offenders-return-to-prison-within-three-years.

10. Audrey Bazos and Jessica Hausman, "Correctional Education as a Crime Control Program," http://www.ceanational.org/PDFs/ed-as-crime-control.pdf.

11. "Confronting Confinement: Final Report of the Commission on Safety and Abuse in American Prisons" (Washington, D.C.: Vera Institute of Justice, 2005), 11.

12. Bureau of Prisons, "Growing Inmate Crowding Negatively Affects Inmates, Staff, and Infrastructure" (Washington, D.C.: Government Accounting Office, September 2012), http://www.gao.gov/products/GAO-12-743.

13. Dwayne Betts, *A Question of Freedom: A Memoir of Learning, Survival, and Coming of Age in Prison* (New York: Penguin, 2009), 182.

14. Michelle Fine et al., "Changing Minds: The Impact of College in a Maximum-Security Prison," September 2001, 21, http://www.prisonpolicy.org/scans/changing_minds.pdf.

15. Laura Winterfield et al., "The Effects of Postsecondary Correctional Education: Final Report," Urban Institute, May 2009, http://www.urban.org/sites/default/files/alfresco/publication-pdfs/411954-The-Effects-of-Postsecondary-Correctional-Education.PDF.

16. "Confronting Confinement," cover.

17. Lynne M. Vieraitis, Tomislav V. Kovandzic, and Thomas B. Marvell, "The Criminogenic Effects of Imprisonment: Evidence from State Panel Data, 1974–2002," *Criminology and Public Policy* 6, no. 3 (August 2007): 589–622.

18. Fine et al., "Changing Minds," 26.

19. *The Words of Martin Luther King, Jr.*, 2nd ed. (New York: William Morrow Paperback, 2001), 19.

20. Jon Marc Taylor, "Alternative Funding Options for Post-Secondary Correctional Education," *Journal of Correctional Education* 56, no. 1 (March 2005): 6.

21. Lois Davis et al., "Evaluating the Effectiveness of Correctional Education," RAND, 2013, http://www.rand.org/pubs/research_reports/RR266.html.

22. Bill Keller, "College for Criminals," *New York Times*, 9 April 2014, http://www.nytimes.com/2014/04/10/opinion/college-for-criminals.html.

23. Jesse McKinley and James C. McKinley Jr., "Cuomo Proposes Higher-Education Initiative in New York Prisons," *New York Times*, 10 January 2016, http://www.nytimes.com/2016/01/11/nyregion/cuomo-proposes-higher-education-initiative-in-new-york-prisons.html.

1: Learning to Learn

1. Conversations with the author.

2. Derek Bok, *Higher Education in America* (Princeton, NJ: Princeton University Press, 2013), 167–69.

3. Derek Bok, "Higher Education Misconceived," *Project Syndicate*, 7 November 2013, https://www.project-syndicate.org/commentary/derek-bok-on-policymakers--misconceptions-of-the-role-of-higher-learning.

4. Harold T. Shapiro, *A Larger Sense of Purpose: Higher Education and Society* (Princeton, NJ: Princeton University Press, 2005), 90.

5. Martha C. Nussbaum, *Cultivating Humanity: A Classical Defense of Reform in Liberal Education* (Cambridge, MA: Harvard University Press, 1997), 9–11.

6. The National Leadership Council for Liberal Education and America's Promise, *College Learning for the New Global Century* (Washington, D.C.: Association of American Colleges and Universities, 2007), 3.

7. Davis et al., "Evaluating," 2–3.

8. Annette Lareau, *Unequal Childhoods: Class, Race, and Family Life* (Berkeley and Los Angeles: University of California Press, 2011); unstructured time, 64; engage in more conversation, 129; encourage success in school, 243.

9. Katherine Long, "Behind Bars, College Is Back in Session in Some Washington Prisons," *Seattle Times*, 21 January 2015, http://www.seattletimes.com/news/behind-bars-college-is-back-in-session-in-some-washington-prisons.

10. "36 Percent of Women in Jail Say They Were Abused as Children," *New York Times*, 12 April 1999, http://www.nytimes.com/1999/04/12/us/36-percent-of-women-in-jail-say-they-were-abused-as-children.html.

11. Conversation with the author.

12. Fine et al., "Changing Minds," 6.

13. Ibid., 5–6.

14. Ibid., 29.

15. "Kenny Johnson, EJP Alumnus," http://educationjustice.net/newsite/stories/johnson_kenny.php.

16. Jorge Heredia, "On Learning Things You've Known Your Whole Life: Social Psychology at San Quentin," *Prison University Project Newsletter* 4, no. 2 (August 2009): 2.

17. Raymond Roe to the author, 15 October 2015.

18. Conversation with the author.

19. Jon E. Hicks, "Brief Graduation Speech," Holy Cross College Commencement in Westville C.F., 21 May 2015, in possession of the author.

20. Bob Simon, "Maximum Security Education," *CBS: 60 Minutes*, 15 April 2007, http://bpi.bard.edu/60-minutes/.

21. Ibid.

22. Beth Schwartzapfel, "Obama Is Reinstating Pell Grants for Prisoners," *Huffpost Politics*, 30 July 2015, http://www.huffingtonpost.com/entry/obama -pell-grants-prisoners_us_55ba7d42e4b0d4f33a020694.

23. Daniel Berthold, "Philosophy Behind Bars: How I Discovered What It Meant to Be a Philosopher After Twenty-Eight Years of Being a Philosopher," unpublished essay.

24. Conversations with the author.

2: Of Value to All

1. David Gonzales, "Faces in the Rubble," *New York Times*, 21 August 2009, http://www.nytimes.com/2009/08/23/nyregion/23bronx.html.

2. Anthony Cardenales, email to author, 9 February 2015; and Adrian Nicole LeBlanc, *Random Family: Love, Drugs, Trouble, and Coming of Age in the Bronx* (New York: Scribner, 2003).

3. Swapna Venugopal Ramaswamy, "Not Bound by the Past: Nonprofits Help Inmates Earn a Second Chance," *Poughkeepsie Journal*, 28 March 2014, http://www.poughkeepsiejournal.com/story/news/2014/03/28/not -bound-by-the-past-nonprofits-help-inmates-earn-a-second-chance/6979257.

4. "Compensation Today," *Pay Scale*, http://www.payscale.com/compensa tion-today/2010/05/hr-guide-to-hiring-felons.

5. Trymaine Lee, "Recidivism Hard to Shake for Ex-offenders Returning Home to Dim Prospects," *Huffington Post*, 10 June 2012, http://www.huffing tonpost.com/2012/06/09/recidivism-harlem-convicts_n_1578935.html.

6. Devah Pager, *Marked: Race, Crime, and Finding Work in an Era of Mass Incarceration* (Chicago: University of Chicago Press, 2007).

7. Michelle Natividad Rodriquez and Beth Avery, "Ban the Box: U.S. Cities, Counties, and States Adopt Fair Hiring Policies, *National Employment Law Project, Toolkit*, 18 April 2016, http://www.nelp.org/publication/ban-the -box-fair-chance-hiring-state-and-local-guide.

8. Lee, "Recidivism."

9. *Who Pays? The True Costs of Incarceration on Families*, September 2015, 20, http://ellabakercenter.org/sites/default/files/downloads/who-pays.pdf.

10. The Pew Charitable Trusts, "Collateral Costs: Incarceration's Effect on Economic Mobility" (Washington, D.C.: Pew Charitable Trusts, 2010), 12, http://www.pewtrusts.org/~/media/legacy/uploadedfiles/pcs_assets/2010 /collateralcosts1pdf.pdf.

11. Conversation with the author.

12. Email to the author.

13. Email to the author.

14. John Schmitt and Kris Warner, "Ex-offenders and the Labor Market," Center for Economic and Policy Research, November 2010, http://cepr.net/documents/publications/ex-offenders-2010-11.pdf.

15. Matthew R. Durose, Alexia D. Cooper, and Howard N. Snyder, "Recidivism of Prisoners Released in 30 States in 2005: Patterns from 2005 to 2010," U.S. Department of Justice, April 2014, http://www.bjs.gov/content/pub/pdf/rprts05p0510.pdf.

16. Baylor Institute for Studies in Religion Special Report, "Recidivism Reduction and Return on Investment: An Empirical Assessment of the Prison Entrepreneurship Program," 2013, http://www.pep.org/baylor-study.

17. "A New Approach to Violence Treatment: An Interview with Dr. James Gilligan," *PsychAlive*, n.d., http://www.psychalive.org/a-new-approach-to-violence-treatment-an-interview-with-dr-james-gilligan.

18. Danielle Kaeble, Lauren Glaze, Anastasios Tsoutis, and Todd Minton, "Correctional Populations in the United States, Bulletin," U.S. Department of Justice, Bureau of Justice Statistics, December 2015, http://www.bjs.gov/content/pub/pdf/cpus14.pdf.

19. Roy Walmsley, *World Prison Population List*, 11th ed., Institute for Criminal Policy Research, http://www.prisonstudies.org/sites/default/files/resources/downloads/world_prison_population_list_11th_edition.pdf.

20. Western, *Punishment and Inequality*, 3.

21. Pew Charitable Trusts, "One in 100: Behind Bars in America 2008," 3, http://www.pewtrusts.org/~/media/legacy/uploadedfiles/pcs_assets/2008/one20in20100pdf.pdf.

22. Niraj Chokshi, "State Prisons Projected to Grow 3 Percent by 2018," *Washington Post*, 18 November 2014, https://www.washingtonpost.com/blogs/govbeat/wp/2014/11/18/state-prisons-projected-to-grow-3-percent-by-2018.

23. E. Ann Carson, "Prisoners in 2014," U.S. Department of Justice, http://www.bjs.gov/content/pub/pdf/p14.pdf.

24. "Annual Determination of Average Cost of Incarceration: A Notice by the Prisons Bureau," *Federal Register*, 9 March 2015.

25. Christian Henrichson and Ruth Delaney, "The Price of Prisons: What Incarceration Costs Taxpayers," Vera Institute of Justice, January 2012, updated July 2012, http://www.vera.org/sites/default/files/resources/downloads/price-of-prisons-updated-version-021914.pdf.

26. "State of Recidivism: The Revolving Door of America's Prisons," Pew Charitable Trusts, 2011, http://www.pewtrusts.org/~/media/legacy/uploadedfiles/pcs_assets/2011/pewstateofrecidivismpdf.pdf.

27. Henrichson and Delaney, "Price."

28. Maria Schiff, "Examining State Prison Health Care Spending: Cost Drivers and Policy Approaches," *HealthAffairsBlog*, http://healthaffairs.org/blog/2014/11/04/examining-state-prison-health-care-spending-cost-drivers-and-policy-approaches.

29. American Civil Liberties Union, "At America's Expense: The Mass Incarceration of the Elderly" (June 2012), http://www.aclu.org/files/assets/elderlyprisonreport_20120613/pdf.

30. Kevin Johnson and H. Darr Beiser, "Aging Prisoners' Costs Put Systems Nationwide in a Bind," *USA Today*, 11 July 2013, http://www.usatoday.com/story/news/nation/2013/07/10/cost-care-aging-prisoners/2479285.

31. Memorandum, "Top Management and Performance Challenges Facing the Department of Justice," Office of the Inspector General, U.S. Department of Justice, 12 November 2013, https://www.justice.gov/sites/default/files/ag/legacy/2014/01/16/sect3.pdf.

32. Washington State Institute for Public Policy, "Evidence-Based Public Policy Options to Reduce Future Prison Construction, Criminal Justice Costs, and Crime Rates," October 2006, http://www.wsipp.wa.gov/ReportFile/952/Wsipp_Evidence-Based-Public-Policy-Options-to-Reduce-Future-Prison-Construction-Criminal-Justice-Costs-and-Crime-Rates_Full-Report.pdf.

33. Beth Schwartzapfel, "Obama Is Reinstating Pell Grants for Prisoners," Marshall Project, https://www.themarshallproject.org/2015/07/30/obama-is-reinstating-pell-grants-for-prisoners#.NS8CWr6u5.

34. "Gov. Cuomo's Bold Step on Prison Education," *New York Times*, 18 February 2014, Opinion Page, http://www.nytimes.com/2014/02/19/opinion/gov-cuomos-bold-step-on-prison-education.html.

35. Davis et al., "Evaluating."

36. Washington State Institute for Public Policy, "Evidence-Based Public Policy Options to Reduce Future Prison Construction, Criminal Justice Costs, and Crime Rates."

37. Daniel Karpowitz and Max Kenner, "Education as Crime Prevention: The Case for Reinstating Pell Grant Eligibility for the Incarcerated," http://www.prisonpolicy.org/scans/crime_report.pdf.

38. Baylor Institute for Studies in Religion Special Report, "Recidivism Reduction and Return on Investment: An Empirical Assessment of the Prison Entrepreneurship Program."

39. Karpowitz and Kenner, "Education."

40. Wendy Erisman and Jeanne Bayer Contardo, "Learning to Reduce Recidivism: A 50-State Analysis of Postsecondary Correctional Education Policy," November 2005, 10, http://www.ihep.org/sites/default/files/uploads/docs/pubs/learningreducerecidivism.pdf.

41. Mary Ellen Batiuk et al., "Disentangling the Effects of Correctional Education: Are Current Policies Misguided? An Event History Analysis," *Criminal Justice* 5, no. 1 (2005): 60, http://crj.sagepub.com/content/5/1/55.full .pdf+html.

42. Ibid., 55.

43. Kathryn E. McCollister, Michael T. French, and Hai Fang, "The Cost of Crime to Society: New Crime-Specific Estimates for Policy and Program Evaluation," http://www.ncbi.nlm.nih.gov/pmc/articles/PMC2835847.

44. Bazos and Hausman, "Correctional Education."

45. Steven Levitt, "The Effect of Prison Population Size on Crime Rates: Evidence from Prison Overcrowding Litigation," *Quarterly Journal of Economics* 111, no. 2 (May 1996): 319–51.

46. Kate Randall, "US State Prison Population Soars as Education Spending Plummets," 4 November 2014, https://www.wsws.org/en/articles/2014/11 /04/cbpp-n04.html.

47. Thomas G. Mortenson, "State Funding: A Race to the Bottom," American Council on Education (Winter 2012), http://www.acenet.edu/the-presi dency/columns-and-features/Pages/state-funding-a-race-to-the-bottom.aspx.

48. Prerna Anand, "Winners and Losers: Corrections and Higher Education in California," 5 September 2012, http://cacs.org/research/winners-and -losers-corrections-and-higher-education-in-california.

49. Vincent Shiraldi and Jason Ziedenberg, "Cellblocks or Classrooms? The Funding of Higher Education and Corrections and Its Impact on African-American Men," Justice Policy Institute (September 2002), http://www.jus ticepolicy.org/uploads/justicepolicy/documents/02-09_rep_cellblocksclass rooms_bb-ac.pdf.

50. Michael Mitchell and Michael Leachman, "Changing Budget Priorities: State Criminal Justice Reform and Investments in Education," Center on Budget and Policies Priorities, 28 October 2014, http://www.cbpp.org /sites/default/files/atoms/files/10-28-14sfp.pdf.

51. Howard Fischer, "Ducey Seeks $70 Million More for Private Prisons," 3 February 2015, http://tucson.com/news/local/crime/ducey-seeks-millions -more.

52. Mortenson, "State Funding."

53. "The Economics of Higher Education," Report Prepared by the Department of the Treasury with the Department of Education (December 2012), https://www.treasury.gov/connect/blog/Documents/20121212_Economics %20of%20Higher%20Ed_vFINAL.pdf.

54. *Higher Education for American Democracy*, vol. 2 (New York: Harper & Brothers, 1948), 3.

55. David E. Lavin, Richard Alba, and Richard A. Silberstein, *Right Versus Privilege: The Open Admission Experiment at the City University of New York* (New York: Free Press, 1981).

56. David Leonhardt, "Even for Cashiers, College Pays Off," *New York Times*, 25 June 2001, http://wwww.nytimes.com/2011/06/26/Sunday-review /26leonhardt.html.

57. Quoted in Steven Hawkins, "Education vs. Incarceration," *American Prospect*, 6 December 2010, http://prospect.org/article/education-vs-incarceration.

58. Alliance for Excellent Education, "Saving Futures, Saving Dollars: The Impact of Education on Crime Reduction and Earnings," September 2013, http://assets.documentcloud.org/documents/78636/savingfutures.pdf.

59. Allie Bidwell, "State Education Funding Lags Behind Pre-Recession Levels," *U.S. News*, 16 October 2014, http://www.usnews.com/news/articles /2014/10/16/state-education-funding-lags-behind-pre-recession-levels.

60. Quoted in NAACP, "Misplaced Priorities," 15.

61. Hawkins, "Education vs. Incarceration."

62. Marie Gottschalk, *Caught: The Prison State and the Lockdown of American Politics* (Princeton, NJ: Princeton University Press, 2015), chap. 4; and Michael B. Katz and Mark J. Stern, *One Nation Divisible: What America Was and What It Is Becoming* (New York: Russell Sage, 2006), chap. 2.

3: Instilling Purpose, Curbing Violence

1. Karlene Faith with Anne Near, eds., *13 Women: Parables from Prison* (Vancouver: Douglas & McIntyre, 2006), 95–113.

2. Trevor, "A Day in the Life of a Prisoner," *Sociological Images*, 8 July 2015, https://thesocietypages.org/socimages/2015/07/08/a-day-in-the-life -of-a-prisoner.

3. John Irwin, *The Warehouse Prison: Disposal of the New Dangerous Class* (Los Angeles: Roxbury, 2005), 154.

4. Ibid., 155.

5. Wilbert Rideau, *In the Place of Justice: A Story of Punishment and Deliverance* (New York: Knopf, 2010), 64.

6. Jon Marc Taylor, "The Education of Ivan Denisovich," *Journal of Correctional Education* 48, no. 2 (June 1997): 84.

7. Joseph T. Hallinan, *Going up the River: Travels in a Prison Nation* (New York: Random House, 2003), 11.

8. John Lennon, "Help Us Learn in Prison," *New York Times*, 5 April 2015, http://www.nytimes.com/2015/04/13/opinion/a-college-education-for-prisoners.html.

9. Michael G. Santos, *Inside: Life Behind Bars in America* (New York: St. Martin's Griffin, 2006), 280.

10. Jeremy Travis, Bruce Western, and Steve Redburn, eds., *The Growth of Incarceration in the United States: Exploring Causes and Consequences* (Washington, D.C.: National Academies Press, 2014), 188.

11. Adam Gopnik, "The Caging of America: Why Do We Lock Up So Many People?" *New Yorker*, 30 January 2012, http://www.newyorker.com/magazine/2012/01/30/the-caging-of-america.

12. Sol Rodriquez, "A Day in the Life of Three Prisoners in Solitary Confinement," *Solitary Watch: News from a Nation on Lockdown*, 29 June 2012, http://solitarywatch.com/2012/06/29/a-day-in-the-life-of-three-prisoners-in-solitary-confinement.

13. Ted Conover, *Newjack: Guarding Sing Sing* (New York: Vintage Books, 2000), 21.

14. Gresham M. Sykes, *The Society of Captives: A Study of a Maximum Security Prison* (1958; Princeton, NJ: Princeton University Press, 2007), 78–79.

15. Travis et al., eds., *The Growth of Incarceration*, 176.

16. Pamela Colloff, "Michael Morton's Life in Prison, in His Own Words," *Texas Monthly*, 7 July 2014, http://www.texasmonthly.com/articles/michael-mortons-life-in-prison-in-his-own-words/#sthash.9ZITmDyL.dpuf.

17. Christopher Zoukis, "Growing Up in Prison: What I've Learned During My Eight Years of Incarceration," *The Blog: Huffpost Crime*, 30 July 2014, http://www.huffingtonpost.com/christopher-zoukis/growing-up-in-prison-what_b_5632218.html.

18. Santos, *Inside*, 122.

19. Conversation with the author, 19 April 2016.

20. Jon Marc Taylor, "The Education of Ivan Denisovich," *Journal of Correctional Education* 48, no. 2 (June 1997): 84.

21. Fine et al., "Changing Minds," 21.

22. Email to the author.

23. Prison University Project, "Featured Students," http://www.prisonuniversityproject.org/student/sean-simms (no longer online but available through the Internet Archive).

24. "Confronting Confinement: A Report of the Commission on Safety and Abuse in American Prisons" (New York: Vera Institute, 2006), 20.

25. "Education from the Inside Out: The Multiple Benefits of College Programs in Prison," (New York: Correctional Association of New York, 2009), iii.

26. Ibid., 8.

27. Fine et al., "Changing Minds," 21.

28. Gopnik, "The Caging of America."

29. Raymond Roe, email to author, 18 July 2015.

30. Amme Voz, "I Thought I'd Escaped Poverty. Then I Went to Prison," *The Nation*, 13 July 2015, http://www.thenation.com/article/i-thought-id-es caped-poverty.

31. Conover, *Newjack*, 83, 95.

32. "Confronting Confinement," 19–20.

33. Ibid., 14.

34. Bureau of Prisons, "Growing Inmate Crowding Negatively Affects Inmates, Staff, and Infrastructure" (Washington, D.C.: Government Accounting Office, September 2012), http://www.gao.gov/products/GAO-12-743.

35. Michael McLaughlin, "Overcrowding in Federal Prisons Harms Inmates, Guards: GAO Report," *Huffington Post*, 14 September 2012, http://www.huffingtonpost.com/2012/09/14/prison-overcrowding-report_n_188 3919.html.

36. David Skarbek, *The Social Order of the Underworld: How Prison Gangs Govern the American Penal System* (New York: Oxford, 2014), 7–9.

37. "Confronting Confinement," 8, 14.

38. Conover, *Newjack*, 98.

39. Ibid., 94.

40. Keith R. Lansdowne, "Choosing Sanity," in *The Funhouse Mirror: Reflections on Prison*, ed. Robert Ellis Gordon and Inmates from the Washington Corrections System (Pullman: Washington State University Press, 2000), 41.

41. "Confronting Confinement," 28.

42. Prison University Project, "Featured Students," http://www.prison universityproject.org/student/aly-tamboura (no longer online but available through the Internet Archive).

43. James Gilligan, *Preventing Violence* (New York: Thames & Hudson, 2001), 98.

44. Winthrop Wetherbee, "Cornell at Auburn: An Experiment in Teaching and Learning," http://cpep.cornell.edu/about-us/our-history.

45. Conversation with the author.

46. Jon E. Hicks, "Hey Sugar, Take a Walk on the Wild Side," Sociology 225 paper, 13 March 2015, in the author's possession.

47. Wesley Caines, email to the author, 25 August 2015.

48. Winterfield et al., "Postsecondary Correctional Education."

49. Shadd Maruna, *Making Good: How Ex-Convicts Reform and Rebuild*

Their Lives (Washington, D.C.: American Psychological Association, 2001); Robert J. Sampson and John H. Laub, *Crime in the Making: Pathways and Turning Points Through Life* (Cambridge, MA: Harvard University Press, 1993); and John H. Laub and Robert J. Sampson, *Shared Beginnings, Divergent Lives: Delinquent Boys to Age 70* (Cambridge, MA: Harvard University Press, 2003).

50. Weatherbee, "Cornell at Auburn."

51. Taylor, "A Day in the Life," 84.

52. Quoted in "Obama Is Reinstating Pell Grants for Prisoners," https://www.themarshallproject.org/2015/07/30/obama-is-reinstating -pell-grants-for-prisoners.

53. Fine et al., "Changing Minds," 21.

54. Winterfield et al., "Postsecondary Correctional Education," 6.

55. Stephen J. Meyer et al., "Implementing Postsecondary Academic Programs in State Prisons: Challenges and Opportunities," *Journal of Correctional Education* 61, no. 2 (June 2010): 166–67.

4: Families and Neighborhoods

1. Stanley Richards, "College for Cons: Still Imperative," *New York Daily News*, 10 April 2014, http://www.nydailynews.com/opinion/college-cons -imperative-article-1.1751197.

2. Gloria Pazmino, *Politico New York*, 21 May 2015, http://www.politico .com/states/new-york/city-hall/story/2015/05.

3. Susan Phillips and Barbara Bloom, "In Whose Best Interest? The Impact of Changing Public Policy on Relatives Caring for Children with Incarcerated Parents," *Child Welfare* 77, no. 5 (1998): 539.

4. Todd R. Clear, *Imprisoning Communities: How Mass Incarceration Makes Disadvantaged Neighborhoods Worse* (New York: Oxford, 2007), 95.

5. Bruce Western and Becky Petit, "Collateral Costs: Incarceration's Effect on Economic Mobility" (Washington, D.C.: Pew Charitable Trusts, 2010), 4.

6. "Children and Families of the Incarcerated Fact Sheet," National Resource Center on Children & Families of the Incarcerated, Rutgers University, https://nrccfi.camden.rutgers.edu/files/nrccfi-fact-sheet-2014.pdf.

7. Christopher J. Mumola, "Incarcerated Children and Their Parents," Bureau of Justice Statistics Special Report, U.S. Department of Justice (August 2000), 2, http://www.bjs.gov/content/pub/pdf/iptc.pdf.

8. Western and Petit, "Collateral Costs," 3.

9. Donald Braman, *Doing Time on the Outside: Incarceration and Family Life in Urban America* (Ann Arbor: University of Michigan Press, 2007), 155.

10. Nancy G. La Vigne, Elizabeth Davies, and Diana Brazzell, "Broken Bonds: Understanding and Addressing the Needs of Children with Incarcerated Parents" (Washington, D.C.: Urban Institute, 2008), 2.

11. U.S. Department of Health and Human Services, "2015 Poverty Guidelines," https://aspe.hhs.gov/2015-poverty-guidelines.

12. *Who Pays?*, 7.

13. Ibid., 14.

14. Lauren-Brooke Eisen, "Paying for Your Time: How Charging Inmates Fees Behind Bars May Violate the Excessive Fines Clause," Brennan Center for Justice, New York University School of Law, 31 July 2014, https://www.brennancenter.org/states-pay-stay-charges.

15. Braman, *Doing Time on the Outside*, 156.

16. *Who Pays?*, 18.

17. Western and Petit, "Collateral Costs," 12.

18. S.E. Siennick, E.A. Stweart, and J. Staff, "Explaining the Association Between Incarceration and Divorce," *Criminology* 52 (2014): 371–98; and Dara Lind, "Every Year of a Prison Term Makes a Couple 32 Percent More Likely to Divorce," *Vox Criminal Justice*, 29 May 2014, http://www.vox.com/2014/5/29/5756646/every-year-of-a-prison-term-makes-a-couple-32-percent-more-likely-to.

19. Donatella Lorch, "Prison Marriages Are on the Increase, Despite Daunting Rates of Failure," *New York Times*, 5 September 1996, http://www.nytimes.com/1996/09/05/nyregion/prison-marriages-are-on-the-increase-despite-daunting-rates-of-failure.html.

20. Creasie Finney Hairston, "The Effect of Incarceration and Reentry on Children, Families, and Communities," *Prisoners and Families: Parenting Issues During Incarceration*, U.S. Department of Health and Human Services, December 2001, https://aspe.hhs.gov/basic-report/prisoners-and-families-parenting-issues-during-incarceration.

21. "Prison Wives and Families and the Stages of Loss and Grief," blog by KK, 21 June 2014, http://www.strongprisonwives.com/magazine/read/prison-wives--families--the-stages-of-loss--grief_410.html.

22. "When a Parent Goes to Prison, a Child Also Pays a Price," *All Things Considered*, National Public Radio, 8 June 2014, http://www.npr.org/2014/06/08/320071553/when-a-parent-goes-to-prison-a-child-also-pays-a-price.

23. U.S. Department of Health and Human Services, Section 4.2.4, "Incarceration and the Family: A Review of Research and Promising Approaches for Serving Fathers and Families," https://aspe.hhs.gov/legacy-page/incarcer

ation-family-review-research-promising-approaches-serving-fathers-families
-effects-parental-incarceration-children-146371.

24. Todd Clear and Natasha A. Frost, *The Punishment Imperative: The Rise and Failure of Mass Incarceration in America* (New York: New York University Press, 2013), 98.

25. Joyce Arditti, *Parental Incarceration and the Family: Psychological and Social Effects of Imprisonment on Children, Parents, and Caregivers* (New York: New York University Press, 2012), 104.

26. Fine et al., "Changing Minds," 27–28.

27. Lili Farhang for Human Impact Partners, "Turning on the TAP: How Returning Access to Tuition Assistance for Incarcerated People Improves the Health of New Yorkers," Oakland, CA, 12 May 2015, 34, http://www.turnon thetapny.org/docs/HIP_TAP_Report_final.pdf.

28. Ibid.

29. La Vigne et al., "Broken Bonds," 7–8.

30. David Murphey and P. Mae Cooper, "Parents Behind Bars: What Happens to Their Children?" *Child Trends*, October 2015, 7, http://www.child trends.org/wp-content/uploads/2015/10/2015-42parents BehindBars.pdf.

31. Ross D. Parke and K. Alison Clarke-Stewart, "From Prison to Home: The Effect of Incarceration and Reentry on Children, Families, and Communities: Effects of Parental Incarceration on Young Children," December 2001, https://aspe.hhs.gov/basic-report/effects-parental-incarceration-young-children.

32. Western and Petit, "Collateral Costs," 21.

33. Human Impact Partners, "Turning on the TAP," 8.

34. "How College Divides Us," *National Journal*, as reported on *Fusion*, 10 December 2013, http://fusion.net/story/4383/how-college-divides-us.

35. Conversation with the author.

36. William Edward Burghardt Du Bois, *The Souls of Black Folk: Essays and Sketches* (A.C. McClurg & Company, 1907), 79.

37. Elijah Anderson, *Codes of the Street: Decency, Violence, and the Moral Life of the Inner City* (New York: W.W. Norton, 1999), 145–46.

38. John Hagan and Ronit Dinovitzer, "Collateral Consequences of Imprisonment for Children, Communities, and Prisoners" *Crime & Justice* 26 (1999): 132–33; and Orlando Patterson, "The Social and Cultural Matrix of Black Youth," in *The Cultural Matrix: Understanding Black Youth*, ed. Orlando Patterson with Ethan Fosse (Cambridge, MA: Harvard University Press, 2015), 115.

39. Francis X. Clines, "Ex-Inmates Urge Return to Areas of Crime to Help," *New York Times*, 23 December 1992, http://www.nytimes.com/1992/12/23/nyregion/ex-inmates-urge-return-to-areas-of-crime-to-help.html.

40. David Gonzalez, "With an Ex-Inmate's Help, Returning to Life Outside," *New York Times*, 7 April 2008, http://www.nytimes.com/2008/04/07/nyregion/07citywide.html.

41. Ibid.

42. Fine et al., "Changing Minds," 2.

5: Democracy and Education

1. Conversations with the author.

2. Glynnis MacNicol, "Rethinking the Justice System for Young People and Revitalizing a Community, Brownsville Project Brings the Accused Before Neighborhood Youth Panels," https://www.chase.com/news/062615-brownsville-1.

3. Ibid.

4. Thomas Ehrlich, ed., *Civic Responsibility and Higher Education* (Westport, CT: Oryx Press, 2000), vi.

5. Ibid., xxvi.

6. Conversation with the author.

7. Conversation with the author.

8. Conversation with the author.

9. David Basile, Prison University Project, Student Portrait, http://www.prisonuniversityproject.org/student/david-basile (no longer online but available through the Internet Archive).

10. Anya Kamenetz, "A Former Drug Dealer Gives a Great Defense of the Liberal Arts," National Public Radio, 21 June 2014, http://www.npr.org/sections/ed/2014/21/315235978/a-former.

11. Email to the author.

12. Fine et al., "Changing Minds," 32.

13. Hicks, "Brief Graduation Speech."

14. Glenn E. Martin, "Leading with Conviction: One Man's Journey to Freedom and Justice," *Huffington Post*, 23 February 2015, updated 25 April 2016.

15. Conversations with and emails to the author.

16. Staci Wilson, "Former Inmate Warns At-Risk Kids," *IndependentWeekender.com*, 20 February 2013 (no longer online but available through newspaper archive).

17. Phone conversation with the author.

18. Dana Boone, "Liberal Arts in Prison," *Grinnell Magazine*, Summer 2014, https://gallery.mailchimp.com/11ecab57ddcd38c804ced9ba9/files/GrinnellMagazinePrisonProgramSummer2015.pdf.

19. Conversations with the author.

20. David Register, "Our Prison Debate Team Beat Harvard's: Here's How We Did It," *The Guardian*, 8 October 2015, http://www.theguardian.com/commentisfree/2015/oct/08/bard-debate-prison-team-beat-harvards-heres-how-we-did-it.

21. Ibid.

22. Jeff Manza and Christopher Uggen, *Locked Out: Felon Disenfranchisement and American Democracy* (New York: Oxford, 2008), 9.

23. "Restoring Voting Rights," Brennan Center for Justice, New York University Law School, https://www.brennancenter.org/issues/restoring-voting-rights.

24. Subuk Hasnain, "12 Jobs You Can't Get with a Felony," *The Chicago Reporter*, 27 January 2015, http://chicagoreporter.com/12-jobs-you-can-get-with-a-felony.

25. Judith N. Shklar, *American Citizenship: The Quest for Inclusion* (Cambridge, MA: Harvard University Press, 1991), 3.

26. Christopher Uggen and Jeff Manza, "Voting and Subsequent Crime and Arrest: Evidence from a Community Sample," *Columbia Human Rights Law Review* 36 (2004–5): 195 ff., http://as.nyu.edu/docs/IO/3858/Voting_and_Subsequent_Crime_and_Arrest.pdf.

27. Conversation with the author.

6: The Challenge of College in Prison

1. Robert Martinson, "What Works? Questions and Answers About Prison Reform," *The Public Interest* (spring 1974): 25, http://www.nationalaffairs.com/doclib/20080527_197403502whatworksquestionsandanswersaboutprisonreformrobertmartinson.pdf.

2. Robert Martinson, "Prison Notes of a Freedom Rider," *Nation* 194 (1962), http://www.thenation.com/article/may-21-1961-famously-hospitable-southerners-greet-freedom-riders-death-threats-and-riots.

3. Rick Sarre, "Beyond 'What Works?' A 25 Year Jubilee Retrospective of Robert Martinson," 3, http://www.aic.gov.au/media_library/conferences/hcpp/sarre.pdf.

4. Marie Gottschalk, *The Prison and the Gallows: The Politics of Mass Incarceration in America* (Cambridge: Cambridge University Press, 2006), 43.

5. Ibid.

6. Thomas Jefferson, "A Bill for Proportioning Crimes and Punishments" (1778), paragraph 3, http://press-pubs.uchicago.edu/founders/documents/amendVIIIs10.html.

7. Rebecca M. McLennan, *The Crisis of Imprisonment: Protest, Politics, and the Making of the American Penal State, 1776–1941* (Cambridge: Cambridge University Press, 2008) 33, 37.

8. Quoted in Alyn Brodsky, *Benjamin Rush: Patriot and Physician* (New York: Macmillan, 2004), 302.

9. Harry Elmer Barnes, "Historical Origin of the Prison System in America," *Journal of Criminal Law and Criminology* 12, no. 1 (1921): 48.

10. "Report on the Prisons and Reformatories of the United States and Canada, Made to the New York Legislature," January 1867 (the quotes are on 47, 144, and 237), https://archive.org/stream/reportonprisonsr00corruoft #page/286/mode/2up.

11. Blake McKelvey, *American Prisons: A History of Good Intentions* (Montclair, NJ: Patterson Smith, 1977), 90.

12. "History of Elmira CF: Nation's First Reformatory," http://www.coreec tionhistory.org/html/chronicl/docs2day/elmira.

13. Alexander W. Pisciotta, *Benevolent Repression: Social Control and the American Reformatory-Prison Movement* (New York: New York University Press, 1994), 53, 54.

14. Quoted in Dana M. Britton, *At Work in the Iron Cage: The Prison as Gendered Organization* (New York: New York University Press, 2003), 28.

15. "History of Bedford Hills Correctional Facility," http://www.reocities .com/MotorCity/Downs/3548/facility/bedford.html.

16. Maude E. Miner, *Slavery of Prostitution: A Plea for Emancipation* (New York: Macmillan, 1916), 231.

17. Nicole Hahn Rafter, *Partial Justice: Women in State Prisons, 1800–1935* (Boston: Northeastern University Press, 1985), 69–74.

18. Thomas Mott Osborne, *Within Prison Walls* (New York: D. Appleton & Co., 1915), 7.

19. McLellan, *The Crisis of Imprisonment*, 335; Osborne, *Within Prison Walls*, chap. 13; and Thomas Mott Osborne, *Society and Prisons: Some Suggestions for a New Penology* (New Haven, CT: Yale University Press, 1924), 137.

20. McLennan, *The Crisis of Imprisonment*, 347.

21. Frank Tannenbaum, *Osborne of Sing Sing* (Chapel Hill: University of North Carolina Press, 1933), 82.

22. McLellan, *The Crisis of Imprisonment*, chap. 8.

23. Ibid., 122.

24. Quoted in ibid., 62.

25. Quoted in Joseph F. Spillane, *Coxsackie: The Life and Death of Prison Reform* (Baltimore: Johns Hopkins University Press, 2014), 33.

26. Ibid., 20.

27. Ibid., 25–26.

28. Ibid., 106.

29. Ibid., 108–9.

30. Ibid., 79

31. Ibid., 96

32. Ibid., 111.

33. Eric Cummins, *The Rise and Fall of California's Radical Prison Movement* (Stanford, CA: Stanford University Press, 1994), 65.

34. Ibid., 22.

35. Ibid.

36. David J. Rothman, "Prisons: The Failure Model," *The Nation*, 21 December 1974, p. 657.

37. Jerome G. Miller, "The Debate on Rehabilitating Criminals: Is It True that Nothing Works?" *Washington Post*, March 1989, http://www.prisonpol icy.org/scans/rehab.html.

38. Robert Martinson, "New Findings, New Views: A Note of Caution Regarding Sentencing Reform," *Hofstra Law Review* 7, no. 2 (1979): 244 and 254.

39. Robert Perkinson, *Texas Tough: The Rise of America's Prison Empire* (New York: Metropolitan Books/Henry Holt, 2010), 362–63.

8: Variety and Difference

1. Kyle Stokes, "What Indiana Will Miss with the State Prisons' College Programs Gone," State Impact: A Reporting Project of WFIU and WTIU, 4 July 2012, http://indianapublicmedia.org/stateimpact/2012/07/04/what -indiana-will-miss-with-the-state-prisons-coll.

2. Conversation with the author.

3. Lois M. Davis et al., "How Effective Is Correctional Education, and Where Do We Go from Here? The Results of a Comprehensive Evaluation" (Santa Monica, CA: RAND Corporation, 2014), http://www.rand.org/pubs /research_reports/RR564.html.

4. Directory available at: http://prisonstudiesproject.org.

5. U.S. Department of Education, Office of Vocational and Adult Education, "Partnerships Between Community Colleges and Prisons: Providing Workforce Education and Training to Reduce Recidivism" (Washington, D.C.: Government Printing Office, 2009), 1, 3.

6. Prison University Project, "About Us: Mission and Goals," https://prison universityproject.org/mission.

7. Phyllis Wentworth, "Massachusetts Can Lead in Inmate College Education: Reviving Pell Grant Program Key First Step," *CommonWealth*, 10 June

2015, http://commonwealthmagazine.org/criminal-justice/massachusetts-can
-lead-in-inmate-college-education.

8. "Texas Spends Millions on College for Prison Inmates," *Statesman*, 22
March 2011, http://www.statesman.com/news/news/state-regional-govt-poli
tics/texas-spends-millions-on-college-for-prison-inma-1/nRYYQ.

9. Jeanne Contardo and Michelle Tolbert, "Prison Postsecondary Education: Bridging Learning from Incarceration to the Community," 5, https://
www.dllr.state.md.us/adulted/aeprisonpostseced.pdf.

10. Ibid., 6.

11. Carla Rivera, "Four Prisons in California to Get Community College
Programs," *Los Angeles Times*, 5 August 2005, http://www.latimes.com/local
/education/la-me-pell-inmate-column-20150805-story.html.

12. U.S. Department of Education, "Partnerships," 10–11.

13. Christopher Zoukis, "North Carolina Community Colleges," *Prison
Education.com*, 2 June 2014, http://www.prisoneducation.com/prison-educa
tion-news/north-carolina-community-colleges-pep.html.

14. U.S. Department of Education, "Partnerships," 10.

15. "Pathways from Prison to Postsecondary Education Project," Vera Institute for Justice, http://www.vera.org/sites/default/files/overview-pathways
-v2.pdf.

16. Keith Collier, "First Seminary Prison Program in Texas Graduates 33
Inmates," *Southwestern Baptist Seminary*, 13 May 2015, http://swbts.edu
/campus-news/news/releases/first-seminary-prison.

17. Erik Eckholm, "Bible College Helps Some at Louisiana Prison Find
Peace," *New York Times*, 5 October 2013, http://www.nytimes.com/2013/10
/06/us/bible-colllege-helps-some.

18. "Master's in Professional Studies," New York Theological Seminary,
http://www.nyts.edu/prospective-students/academic-programs/master-of
-professional-studies.

19. http://www.educationjustice.net/home.

20. Inside-Out Center, "About Us," Temple University, http://www.inside
outcenter.org/about-us.html.

21. Maurice Chammah, "Starting New Businesses Behind Bars Creates an
Incentive for Texas Inmates," *New York Times*, 16 February 2013, http://www
.nytimes.com/2013/02/17/us/entrepreneurship-program-for-texas-inmates
.html.

22. Byron Johnson, William Wubbenhorst, and Curtis Schraeder, "Recidivism Reduction and Return on Investment: An Empirical Assessment of the
Prison Entrepreneurship Program," 18, www.pep.org/baylor-study.

23. U.S. Department of Education, "Partnerships," 7.

24. Thomas R. Bailey, Shanna Smith Jaggars, and Davis Jenkins, *Redesigning America's Community Colleges: A Clear Path to Student Success* (Cambridge, MA: Harvard University Press, 2015), 5.

25. Jeffrey Jurgens, "The Impact of College-in-Prison Programming on the Educational and Life Experiences of 'Main-Campus' Students," a study conducted for the Consortium for Liberal Arts in Prison, 2013.

26. Conversation with the author.

Conclusion

1. Conversation with the author.

2. Joel and Eric Best, *The Student Loan Mess* (Berkeley: University of California Press, 2014), 48, 95; and Suzanne Mettler, *Degrees of Inequality: How the Politics of Higher Education Sabotaged the American Dream* (New York: Basic Books, 2014), 2.

3. Liz Weston, "OECD: The US Has Fallen Behind Other Countries in College Completion," *Business Insider*, 9 September 2014, http://www.businessinsider.com/r-us-falls-behind-in-college-competition-oecd-2014-9.

4. Georgetown University Center on Education and the Workforce, "Help Wanted," https://cew.georgetown.edu/cew-reports/help-wanted.

5. Debbie Mukamai, Rebecca Silbert, and Rebecca M. Taylor, "Degrees of Freedom: Expanding College Opportunities for Currently and Formerly Incarcerated Californians," February 2015, https://www.law.stanford.edu/publications/degrees-of-freedom-expanding-college-opportunities-for-currently-and-formerly-incarcerated-californians.

6. William C. Symonds, Robert Schwartz, and Ronald F. Ferguson, *Pathways to Prosperity: Meeting the Challenge of Preparing Young Americans for the 21st Century* (Cambridge, MA: Pathways to Prosperity Project, Harvard University Graduate School of Education, 2011), 2.

7. Claudia Goldin and Lawrence F. Katz, *The Race Between Education and Technology* (Cambridge, MA: Harvard University Press, 2008), 350–51 (for the quotes).

8. Michael D. Shear, "Obama Speech Ties U.S. Need for More College Graduates to the Economic Recovery," *Washington Post*, 9 August 2010, http://www.washingtonpost.com/wp-dyn/content/article/2010/08/09/AR2010080904278.html.

9. "Remarks by the President in State of the Union Address," 20 January 2015, https://www.whitehouse.gov/the-press-office/2015/01/20/remarks-president-state-union-address-january-20-2015.

10. "Toward a New Focus on Outcomes in Higher Education, Remarks by Secretary Arne Duncan at the University of Maryland–Baltimore County," 27 July 2015, http://www.ed.gov/new/speeches/toward-new-focus -outcomes-higher-education.

11. Summers and Balls, "Report," 137.

12. Allie Bidwell, "Critics Pan Obama's Community College Plan," *U.S. News*, 9 January 2015, http://www.usnews.com/news/articles/2015/01/09 /critics-pan-obamas-community-college-plan.

13. Campaign for Free College Tuition, "Promise Programs: Making Free College Tuition a Reality," http://www.freecollegenow.org/making_free_col lege_tuition_a_reality.

14. Tennessee Promise, "Frequently Asked Questions," https://www.in sidehighered.com/sites/default/server_files/files/TN%20Promise%20FAQ .pdf.

15. "City Colleges of Chicago: Chicago Star Scholarships," http://www.ccc .edu/departments/Pages/chicago-star-scholarship.aspx.

16. "U.S. Department of Education Launches Second Chance Pell Pilot Program for Incarcerated Individuals," 31 July 2015, http://www.ed.gov/news /press-releases/us-department-education-launches-second-chance-pell-pilot -program-incarcerated-individuals.

17. "Why Republicans Should Support Obama's Pell Grants for Prisoners," *NJ Star-Ledger*, http://www.nj.com/opinion/index.ssf/2015/08/why_republi cans_should_support_obamas_pell_grants.html.

18. Loretta Lynch and Arne Duncan, "To Cut Crime, Turn Jailbirds into Book Worms," *USA Today*, 3 August 2015, http://www.usatoday.com /story/opinion/2015/08/03/loretta-lynch-arne-duncan-education-matters -column/31021953.

19. "For Prisoners, a Path to Society," *New York Times*, 31 July 2015, http:// www.nytimes.com/2015/08/01/opinion/for-prisoners-a-path-to-society.html.

20. "Alexander's Statement on Administration Plan to Give Pell Grants to Prisoners," 31 July 2015, http://www.help.senate.gov/chair/newsroom/press /alexander-statement-on-administration-plan-to-give-pell-grants-to-prisoners.

21. Jennifer C. Kerr, "Obama to Extend College Aid Grants to Some Prison Inmates," AP, 31 July 2015, http://bigstory.ap.org/articles/5631416602ae4f98 b2dd6d9da10eb8a.

22. Gabrielle Emanuel, "The Plan to Give Pell Grants to Prisoners," *All Things Considered*, National Public Radio, 31 July 2015, http://www.npr.org /sections/ed/2015/07/31/428148089/the-plan-to-give-pell-grants-to-prisoners.

23. Jessica Bakeman, "Republicans Rally Against Cuomo's Prison-College Plan," *Politico New York*, 18 February 2014, http://www.capitalnewyork.com

/article/albany/2014/02/8540470/republicans-rally-against-cuomos-prison
-college-plan.

24. *Congressional Record*, 16 November 1993, 29449–50.

25. Mukamai et al., "Degrees of Freedom," 2.

26. Glenn Kessler, "Do 72 Percent of For-Profit Programs Have Graduates Making Less Than High School Dropouts?" *Washington Post*, 11 April 2014, https://www.washingtonpost.com/news/fact-checker/wp/2014/04/11/the -obama-administrations-claim-that-72-percent-of-for-profits-programs-have -graduates-making-less-than-high-school-dropouts.

27. U.S. Department of Education, "Obama Administration Takes Action to Protect Americans from Predatory, Poor-Performing Career Colleges," 14 March 2014, http://www.ed.gov/news/press-releases/obama-administra tion-takes-action-protect-americans-predatory-poor-performing-ca.

28. Marc Mauer and David Cole, "How to Lock Up Fewer People," *New York Times*, 23 May 2015, http://www.nytimes.com/2015/05/24/opinion/sun day/how-to-lock-up-fewer-people.html.

Index

About the Author

Ellen Condliffe Lagemann is the Levy Institute Research Professor at Bard College, where she is also the Distinguished Fellow in the Bard Prison Initiative. Formerly she served as president of the Spencer Foundation and as dean of the Harvard Graduate School of Education. She lives in Ghent, New York.

Publishing in the Public Interest

Thank you for reading this book published by The New Press. The New Press is a nonprofit, public interest publisher. New Press books and authors play a crucial role in sparking conversations about the key political and social issues of our day.

We hope you enjoyed this book and that you will stay in touch with The New Press. Here are a few ways to stay up to date with our books, events, and the issues we cover:

- Sign up at www.thenewpress.com/subscribe to receive updates on New Press authors and issues and to be notified about local events
- Like us on Facebook: www.facebook.com/newpressbooks
- Follow us on Twitter: www.twitter.com/thenewpress

Please consider buying New Press books for yourself; for friends and family; or to donate to schools, libraries, community centers, prison libraries, and other organizations involved with the issues our authors write about.

The New Press is a 501(c)(3) nonprofit organization. You can also support our work with a tax-deductible gift by visiting www.thenewpress.com/donate.